Slip-Stitch Knitting

Color Pattern
The Easy Way

Roxana Bartlett

Photography, Joe Coca
Technical editing, Dorothy T. Ratigan
Cover design, Elizabeth R. Mrofka
Production, Dean Howes

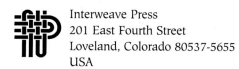
Interweave Press
201 East Fourth Street
Loveland, Colorado 80537-5655
USA

Printed in Hong Kong by Sing Cheong

Library of Congress Cataloging-in-Publication Data:

Bartlett, Roxana, 1939–
    Slip-stitch knitting : color pattern the easy way / by Roxana
Bartlett.
        P.   cm.
    Includes index.
    ISBN 1-883010-32-2
    1. Knitting—Patterns.   I. Title.
TT820.B36 1998
746.43'2—dc21   97-43187
                                                            CIP

First printing: IWP—7.5M:1197:CC
Second printing: IWP—4M:1198:CC

CONTENTS

To my husband, David, and to my good friends,
Maggie and Judy, for their hours of patient listening,
loyal enthusiasm, and cherished advice.

———————————————

Grateful thanks to my editor, Judith Durant,
for all her help on every aspect of the book and
for putting up with the eccentricities of the
artistic temperament and to Ann Budd for working with
meticulous care on the details for which I have little patience—
both now know more about right-side brains than they
ever wanted to. My special thanks to Sharon Dalebout,
Anne Sneary, and Marla Dowell for knitting sample sweaters—
great friends and knitters all.

———————————————

PREFACE

It was nearly a decade ago that I first began to experiment with color patterns made with slip stitches. I love sweaters with many colors and patterns but had always found stranded knitting tedious. No matter how much I admired a beautiful multicolored sweater, the thought of knitting with more than one yarn at a time almost always discouraged me. That is why I was intrigued the moment I discovered the mosaic patterns in Barbara Walker's wonderful *Second Treasury of Knitting Patterns* (Charles Scribner's Sons, 1970). I was amazed to think that a knitter could have so much fun with color while knitting with only one yarn at a time. Slip stitches are surely like the magician's sleight of hand. Even in their simplest form, (*k1, sl 1; repeat from *), slip stitches can work magic with a knitted fabric.

My fascination with this technique led me to work more with Ms. Walker's mosaic patterns, to tell other knitters about the technique, and finally, to design slip-stitch patterns of my own. I hope that you will not only enjoy using my slip-stitch patterns and making the garments I've designed with them, but that through this wonderfully simple technique you will gain the confidence to create your own designs!

INTRODUCTION

Slip-stitch patterns are defined by the interaction of light and dark stitches with one another. Although these patterns may look complicated, they are created by working a sequence of two rows of a light color followed by two rows of a dark color, in a series of knitted (or purled) and slipped stitches. Stitches in the color of the working yarn, say the light color, are knit (or purled), and stitches in the dark color (the color worked in the previous row) are slipped. For example, let's say you are doing a slip-stitch pattern in stockinette stitch and have cast on all your stitches with the dark yarn. To develop the pattern, use the light color and simply knit the stitches you want to be light and slip the stitches you want to be dark. In this way, you can work intricate patterns using only one color at a time.

Consider the second row of a color sequence as a mirror image of the first. If you are working back and forth (i.e., not in the round) in stockinette stitch, all the stitches that were knit in the previous row are purled, and all the stitches that were slipped are slipped again. Because the second row mirrors the first, you don't have to worry about pattern multiples or reading a partly completed chart backwards. Simply work the stitches that were worked on the previous row and slip the stitches that were slipped. You will automatically end up back at the beginning of the chart, ready to work two rows with the next color. For this reason, patterns composed of many motifs are no more difficult than patterns composed of a single motif.

Slip-stitch patterns can be worked just as easily in the round. For the mirror row, simply repeat the first row.

CHAPTER 1

READING CHARTS

Although slip-stitch patterns can be written in text format with instructions to knit and slip so many stitches in a row, they lend themselves better to graphic representation. Charts depicting the shapes of the color pattern are easy to follow. Each square on a slip-stitch chart represents one stitch and each row represents two rows that you work with a single color. Work a slip-stitch chart from right to left for the first row of a two-row sequence, and follow the established pattern for the second row.

Rows are numbered along both sides of the chart. Notice that odd numbers appear on the right and even numbers on the left. The odd numbers identify the first row of each sequence and indicate that the chart is read from right to left. The even numbers, which are on the same row as the odd numbers, represent the second row of each sequence and indicate that a mirror of the previous row should be worked from left to right. The column of squares to the right of the chart indicates which yarn should be used in each row: black squares indicate dark yarn, white squares indicate light yarn. These squares are not part of the slip-stitch pattern and should not be worked as such. In the sample charts, Rows 1 and 2 are both worked with dark yarn, Rows 3 and 4 are worked with light yarn, and so on.

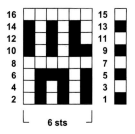

This chart has 6 stitches and 16 rows. Odd-numbered rows are labeled on the right, indicating that the chart is read from right to left for these rows; even-numbered rows are labeled on the left, indicating that the chart is read from left to right for these rows. The column of squares to the right indicates which yarn should be used in each row.

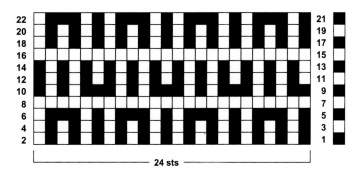

Here is the same chart element repeated over 24 stitches and 22 rows.

Here is the big chart from page 7 knitted up as a swatch.

Slip-stitch patterns can also be knit in the round. To work circularly, follow the first row of a two-row sequence, which is an odd-numbered row, exactly as it is charted, from right to left. For the second row of the sequence, simply repeat the first row

When slipping stitches, always slip them as if to purl so they won't become twisted. To keep yarn carries on the wrong side of the knitting, hold the yarn in back when you are slipping stitches on right-side rows; when slipping stitches on wrong-side rows, hold the yarn in front.

To try out the chart on the previous page, cast on twenty-four stitches with a light yarn and purl one row. Then change to a dark yarn and begin the first row of the chart as follows:

Knit one stitch for each of the black squares and slip one stitch (with yarn held in back) for each of the white squares. On the next row, purl the dark stitches and slip (with yarn in front) the light stitches—the same ones that you slipped on the previous row. Then follow Row 3 of the chart using the light yarn, knitting one stitch for each of the white squares and slipping one stitch for each of the black squares. On the next row, purl the light stitches and slip the dark stitches. Continue alternating light and dark yarns every two rows, working the stitches indicated by the chart to be worked and slipping the others.

CHAPTER 2

WORKING THE CHARTS

Slipped stitches tend to give knitted fabric a slightly rippled texture. Although much of this unevenness disappears when the piece is blocked, enough remains for an interesting surface quality. But you should be aware that slipped stitches tend to spread horizontally when blocked, making it essential that you steam or wash a swatch before using it to determine stitch gauge. Otherwise, your garment may turn out to be several inches wider than intended.

Stockinette and Garter Stitches

You can work slip-stitch patterns in stockinette or garter stitch, and some of the most interesting effects can be achieved by combining the two.

To work a slip-stitch chart back and forth in garter stitch, knit and slip stitches in the first row as described on page 8, then work the second row by knitting the stitches that were knit and slipping the stitches that were slipped. To keep yarn carries on the wrong side of the knitting, remember to hold the working yarn *in front* when slipping stitches on wrong-side rows and hold it *in back* when slipping stitches on right-side rows.

To work a slip-stitch chart circularly in stockinette stitch, knit and slip stitches in

Here, a slip-stitch pattern is worked in stockinette stitch.

The same chart has been used for this swatch as for the one above but here it is worked in a combination of stockinette and garter stitch.

Here the chart from page 9 is worked in all garter stitch.

In this swatch, the green stitches have been worked in garter stitch, further distinguishing them from the red.

the first round of a sequence as described on page 8, then repeat the first round for the second. To work a slip-stitch chart circularly in garter stitch, knit and slip stitches in the first round of a sequence as for stockinette stitch and then work the second round by purling the stitches that were previously knit and slipping the stitches that were previously slipped, remembering to hold the yarn in back when slipping stitches in both rounds.

Working selected stitches in garter stitch may take a bit more time than working only in stockinette stitch, but the enriched surface texture can be well worth the effort. Working a selected element of the design in garter stitch can produce a more interesting, visually striking fabric. Even an occasional garter stitch scattered through a knitted fabric can enhance the overall texture.

Dividing a chart and working some elements in stockinette stitch and others in garter stitch can help to emphasize shapes within the overall pattern and to distinguish between images and fill-in patterns.

Choose a slip-stitch chart and experiment by working it in stockinette stitch, garter stitch, and a combination of the two. Notice how the different pattern stitches change the shapes of the motifs as well as the texture of the knitted surface. As you experiment with slip-stitch patterns, remember that you can make many visual variations simply by substituting different stitches.

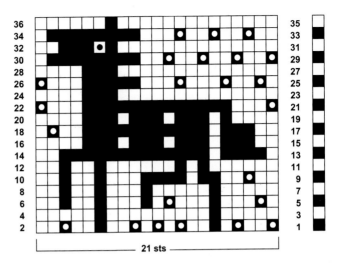

Here, the red stitches of the filler pattern are worked in garter stitch while the red stitches of the horse and the green background stitches are worked in stockinette.

Charts that have dots on some of the squares indicate places in the chart where purl stitches might enhance the surface of the garment.

CHAPTER 3

COLOR

Because slip-stitch patterns involve the play of colors against one another, they are ideal for experiments in color. And because you use only one color at a time, you are free to focus your attention on these explorations, not on keeping track of multiple balls of yarn. Do you have a basket (or two or more) of leftover yarns? Dig in and have fun experimenting with slip-stitch patterns.

If you are intrigued but perhaps a little intimidated by the endless possibilities, take heart. The simplest way to begin color exploration is to choose one color for

One consistent color can serve as an effective background. Here, pale green yarn unites multicolored motifs.

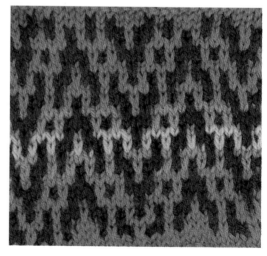

Keeping one color consistent in a slip-stitch pattern creates a visual grid for the overall design. Here, the dark blue is consistent and appears as a design worked with a multicolored background.

either the light or the dark stitches. Then try different colors for the other stitches. Keeping one color consistent in a slip-stitch pattern creates a visual "grid" that holds together and integrates the other colors. One consistent color can also serve as an effective background for images.

When adding a new color, simply cut the old yarn, pick up the new, and continue following the chart as if nothing had happened. But interesting changes *will* happen in the knitting. I usually prefer to change colors on the second row of a two-row sequence. In slip-stitch patterns, shapes are changed on the first row of a sequence. I find the color effects to be more interesting when the color changes don't coincide with the shape changes. Changing

In the top swatch, the color was changed on an odd row, at the same time the pattern changed. I prefer to change color just after a change in shape, as in the bottom swatch. To my eye, this creates a more interesting effect.

Colors that are close in value appear rich when combined.

colors just after a change in the shapes can also form a visual bridge between one element of the pattern and another, further integrating pattern shapes and color.

The best way to determine whether two colors will work together in a slip-stitch pattern is to knit a sample. Although you can get a general feel for color compatibility by holding skeins of yarn together, you won't be able to see how colors interact in the pattern without knitting them. But be forewarned: you can keep yourself busy for years knitting samples of slip-stitch patterns using different yarn and stitch combinations!

Combining colors in a close range of values can make the pattern seem to appear and disappear.

Combining colors that are too close in value may result in loss of definiton.

When used with yarns of very close values, isolated, simple shapes look intriguing on a plain background.

Using two variegated yarns forms surprising combinations of colors and values.

Isolated, simple shapes on a plain background may be stark and less interesting when done with highly-contrasting yarns.

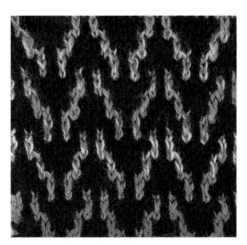

Using a variegated yarn with a plain one enhances both.

Value, or how light or dark a color appears, plays an important role in color interaction. Colors that are close in value can appear visually rich when used in combination. But colors that are too similar in value may lose definition next to one another and obscure the pattern. Combining yarns that have a close range of values can make the pattern shapes seem to appear and disappear, an effect that adds an intriguing visual play to a pattern. A slip-stitch pattern made up of isolated dark shapes against a light background can maintain its integrity even when the colors are quite close in value. On the other hand, such a pattern worked in yarns of highly contrasting value may appear stark and less interesting.

The more colors you incorporate in a slip-stitch pattern, the more interesting the knitting will be. *But* there will be more tails of yarn to weave in when you've fin-

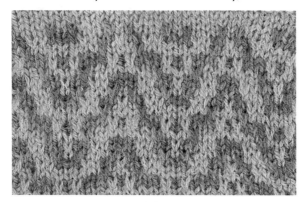

Using two shades or colors together as one yarn can effortlessly add a depth and complexity to simple patterns. In this example, medium blue is combined with light blue for the dark stitches, and pumpkin is combined with beige for the light.

ished knitting. If you work a slip-stitch chart in just one light and one dark yarn, alternating those two yarns every two rows, you can carry the unused yarn up the side of the knitting. However, yarn carries longer than two rows can cause tension problems and may result in puckering at the edges. Therefore, for complex color sequences, you will probably have to cut the yarn at nearly every color change.

If you are so averse to weaving in ends of yarn that you're inclined to abandon color work altogether, consider pairing a solid-colored yarn with a variegated one. Or even pairing two different variegated yarns. You'll get the rich appearance of many colors and the ease of working with only two yarns. Variegated yarns, which tend to knit up in an often unwanted stripe or zigzag pattern in single-color knitting, are ideal for slip-stitch knitting. If you alternate the variegated yarn with a plain yarn, the peculiarities of the variegated yarn are diminished while the uniformity of the plain yarn is enhanced.

Another way to create a rich color effect is to use two shades or colors of light-weight yarn as one yarn. The combination can effortlessly add a depth and complexity to the simplest of patterns.

For the most intricate and complex visual effect, use several colors for both the light and dark parts of the chart. In so doing, you can create bold or subtle color and pattern relationships. Look closely at the color sequences in Fair Isle patterns. In the most complex and successful of these patterns, many colors are used in the motifs as well as in the background. A similar effect is easy to achieve with slip stitches.

To experiment with this idea, progressively change the colors in both the light and dark areas as you work through a charted pattern. Begin your experiment with groups of contrasting colors, such as an assortment of green and purple yarns (or any other colors that appeal to you). Don't be afraid to include a wide variety of shades, hues, and values of greens and purples. Not all combinations will be successful, but you will learn a great deal by working with them.

Work the slip-stitch chart of your choice, using the greens for one part and the purples for the other. As you knit, simply change at random from one green to another and from one purple to another. Remember that by changing the colors on different rows of the chart, you can further enrich the overall effect.

Here, burgundy and plum are used as one for the dark stitches, and blue and green of like values are used for the light.

For the most intricate and complex visual effect, use several colors for both the light and the dark parts of the chart. Here, all the colors used are similar in value.

This swatch uses highly-contrasting yarns.

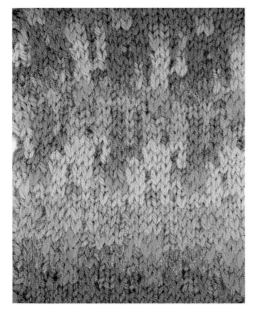

Color value can be the key to successful combinations. Try pairing similar values such as light greens with light purples.

Try pairing contrasting values such as light greens with dark purples, or vice versa.

reversed for the other side. I "filled in" the empty spaces surrounding these rearing horses with dots of color. You can always isolate a single pattern element in this way by surrounding it with a "filler" pattern.

In choosing a charted pattern, consider its size. Although it is technically possible to use a slip-stitch pattern with any number of stitches, the size of the pattern should relate to the size of the garment. A large-scale pattern probably isn't a good choice for small pieces such as socks, hats, and mittens. You don't want the overall scale of the pattern to overwhelm the garment. Garments with large areas for patterning, such as sweaters, are more versatile and can accommodate both large and small patterns. Keep in mind that yarn size is a factor in scale considerations. More repeats or larger images can be fitted into a piece if you use smaller yarn.

Slip-stitch patterns can also be combined with single-color knitting. But remember, the two may knit up to different gauges. If you make adjustments for the two gauges, the combination can be visually appealing. However, if you want your garment to have a vertical band of slip-stitch pattern next to an area worked in a single color, consider knitting the band separately and sewing it on later. Slip-stitch patterns tend to work up to many more rows per inch than single-color knitting, requiring that short rows be worked in the single-colored area if the two are to be worked side by side.

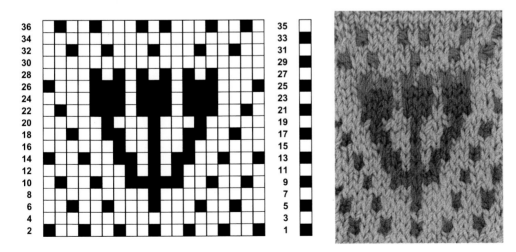

Use "filler" patterns for empty spaces around motifs.

Another possibility is to combine slip-stitch patterns with intarsia. In the Baa, Baa Black Sheep sweater on page 54, I worked one sheep in a contrasting color, lending surprise to the allover pattern with very little extra effort. Don't be afraid to experiment—slip-stitch patterns are so simple to work that they invite innovation and playfulness!

Slip-stitch patterns can be effectively combined with single-color knitting, but you will have to make adjustments for gauge. The first swatch was knit entirely with U.S. 4 needles. For the second swatch I used U.S. 4 needles for the seed stitch and U.S. 6 needles for the slip stitch.

CHAPTER 5

USING SLIP STITCHES IN GARMENTS

I f you want to incorporate a slip-stitch pattern into a garment that already has written instructions, an accurate gauge sample is a must—but then, when isn't it? Once you have established your slip-stitch gauge, find a pattern that calls for that gauge. (Of course, you *could* use a pattern that calls for a different gauge, but that would require a lot of calculation, which we won't go into here.)

To determine how many repeats of the chart can be worked with the total number of stitches called for, divide the stitches for the garment by the number of stitches in the pattern repeat. If the resulting number is not a whole number, the remainder represents the percentage of pattern repeat left over for a partial repeat. When working with partial repeats, center the pattern so that the partial repeats occur at the under-arms or another inconspicuous place.

If you want to work with full repeats only, you will have to adjust the number of stitches. For example, let's assume your sweater instructions call for 210 stitches and you want to use a slip-stitch pattern with a repeat of 12 stitches. To find the number of pattern repeats possible, divide

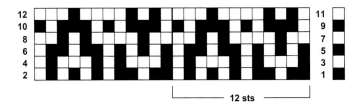

You may want to adjust the number of stitches in a repeat.

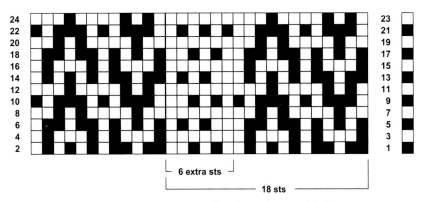

Here, six extra stitches have been added.

210 by 12 for 17.5. To determine the number of stitches required for 17 full repeats, multiply 17 by 12, which is 204. To work only full pattern repeats, you will have to knit your sweater with 204 stitches. Alternately, you can incorporate an extra 6 stitches elsewhere in the pattern, perhaps by working a panel of stripes or dots at the underarms. Either way, such small adjustments to the total stitch count have little effect on finished sweater size.

You may also experiment with knitting your slip-stitch chart at different gauges to get different sizes. As long as

the appearance of the slip-stitch pattern is acceptable to you, this is a simple solution to sizing.

If you want to use only full repeats and do not want to adjust the number of stitches, you can adjust the chart instead. For example, say you want to use a motif with a 17-stitch repeat and your pattern calls for 160 stitches. Adding 3 stitches to the motif makes it a 20-stitch repeat, and your pattern will accommodate eight full repeats. You can work these extra stitches by making a little "filler" pattern of dots between the images.

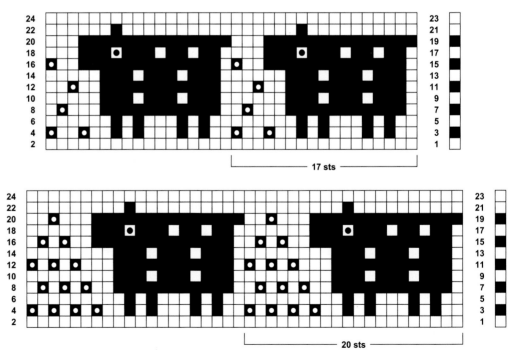

Here, three extra stitches were added to the repeat as filler. (Squares marked with a dot indicate that these stitches could be in garter stitch to add interest.)

I like to shape sleeves knit from the top down with decreases along the underarm "seam" which is rarely in view.

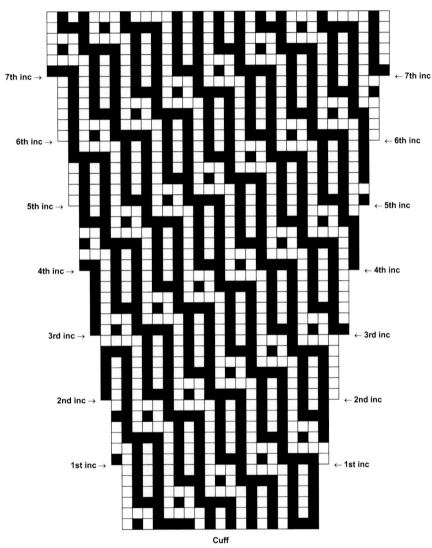

7th inc →   ← 7th inc

6th inc →   ← 6th inc

5th inc →   ← 5th inc

4th inc →   ← 4th inc

3rd inc →   ← 3rd inc

2nd inc →   ← 2nd inc

1st inc →   ← 1st inc

Cuff

For sleeves knit from the bottom up, graphing out the increases can help you visualize what happens to the slip-stitch pattern.

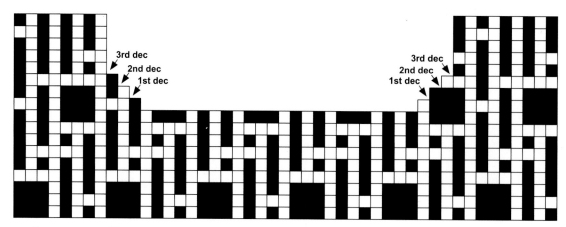

3rd dec
2nd dec
1st dec

3rd dec
2nd dec
1st dec

Shaping a neckline in a slip-stitch pattern is no more complicated than shaping a neckline in single-color knitting.

One row of the background color is worked between the corrugate ribbing and the slip-stitch pattern to give the pattern a ground.

Sleeves also require adjustments to motifs and/or stitch count. I like to join the shoulders of a sweater and then pick up stitches from around the armhole and knit the sleeve downward to the cuff, decreasing stitches along the underarm "seam" to shape the sleeve. A slip-stitch pattern will not match perfectly along the decreases, but because this part of a sweater is almost never in view, I don't consider it a problem. (If a sleeve is knit from the top down with a pattern that has an obvious top and bottom, such as a kitten, you will have to read the chart from the top to the bottom—start with the last row and work down the chart to the first—to avoid an upside-down image.) Sleeves that are knit upward from the cuff require you to add stitches as the sleeve progresses. With each increase, you expand the charted pattern into its next repeat. If this seems confusing, try drawing it out on graph paper. When you can picture what happens in the pattern for a few increases, you will be able to anticipate the rest and probably won't have to draw the entire sleeve. But if you do draw it out, you will have a picture to follow for the second sleeve.

For a neckline, subtract stitches from the slip-stitch pattern. Since the even rows always bring you back to the beginning of a row of pattern, the shaping will be no more complicated than shaping a neckline in single-color knitting.

When knitting a sweater, you may wish to incorporate some pattern colors into the ribbing; simple horizontal stripes, slip-stitch corrugated, or slip-stitch seed make great beginnings. The row that you begin the slip-stitch chart on will depend on the

effect you want. If you are using a chart with an image, then you will most likely wish to work one or more rows of the background color before you begin the first charted row. If the ribbing and the background color are quite different in value, you may want to soften the transition by incorporating a row or two of *k1, sl 1; repeat from * around rather than abruptly change between the ribbing color and background color. In the On the Farm Pullover (page 65), I used this technique twice—just above the ribbing and again at the background color change. If your ribbing is knitted in a dark color and you want a clean look without a light line appearing just above the ribbing where the slip-stitch pattern begins, then start knitting the chart

Two rows of background are worked between the seed-stitch ribbing and the slip-stitch pattern.

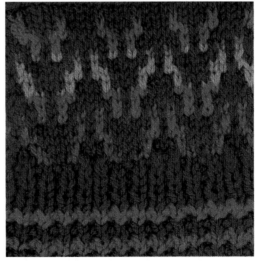

To prevent a light line just above the ribbing, begin the slip-stitch pattern with Row 3 of the chart.

from Row 3, a light-colored row, for the first time through the chart. Otherwise, you'd have to work two rows with the light-colored yarn immediately after the ribbing so it would be there to slip for Row 1 of the chart. When you have worked to the end of the chart, begin on Row 1 for the next repeat. In this way you can introduce the lighter part of the chart gradually without an obtrusive light area.

Whether you begin with a light or dark row is incidental unless the pattern is an image, in which case you begin with the color of the background rows, and that color can be either light or dark.

Slip-Stitch Ribbings

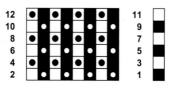

Three-Color Seed Stitch Ribbing
Uneven number of sts
Cast with Color A
Rows 1 and 2. With Color B, *K1, Sl1 repeat from *
Rows 3 and 4. With color C, *Sl1, K1 repeat from *
Rows 5 and 6. With color A, *K1, Sl1 repeat from *

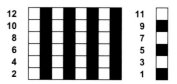

Two-Color Slip-Stitch Corrugated Ribbing
Uneven number of sts
Cast on with Color A
Row 1. With Color B, *K1, Sl1 repeat from *
Row 2. With Color B, *P1, Sl1 repeat from *
Row 3. With color A, *Sl1, K1 repeat from *
Row 4. With color A, *Sl1, P1 repeat from *

CHAPTER 6

COMBINING SLIP-STITCH PATTERNS

When combining patterns from different charts, be sure to consider their relative scale. The overall effect is most successful when a large pattern is combined with a small one, or a complex pattern with a simple one.

By combining slip-stitch patterns in a single garment, you will create a visual complexity that can greatly enhance a simple shape. To decide which patterns work well together, take a few minutes to analyze the basic configuration of each. Are they made up of small, isolated shapes? Bold simple shapes? More complex ones? Do the shapes form strong horizontal bands? Strong diagonal bands?

After you have determined the basic characteristics of the patterns, experiment with combining them. Charts that work well together often have similar shapes that, although different in scale or overall complexity, are a complementary reflection of one another. Often these similarities may derive from one pattern repeating a small element of another larger pattern. On the other hand, if patterns have too many similarities—particularly of scale or complexity—then the combination may be too

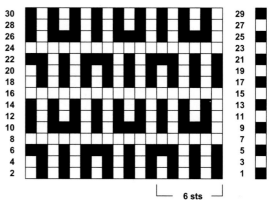

This chart consists of small, isolated shapes.

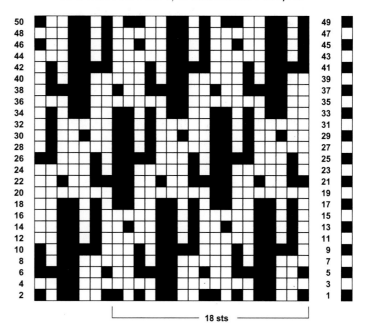

The shapes in this chart are simple and bold.

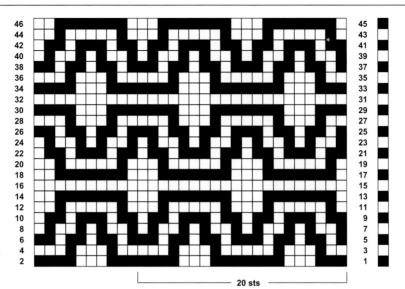

This pattern forms strong horizontal bands.

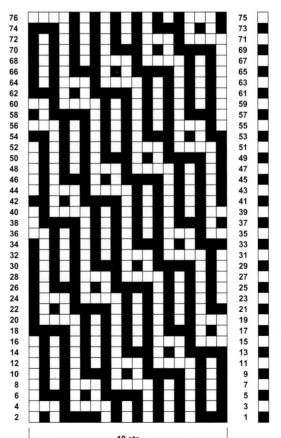

Here is an allover design of diagonal bands.

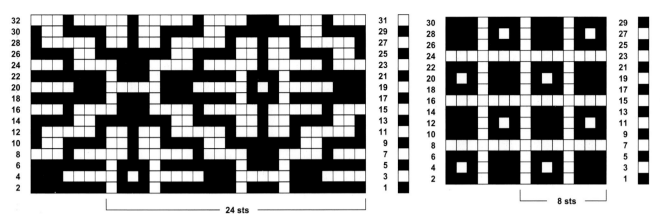

*These two charts will work well together because the one at left incorporates
a small image from the other, that of the simple two-color square.*

repetitious to be pleasing. If you want to add a complementary pattern to your garment and can't find one that is just right, try making up your own very simple pattern from an element of the main chart. Many times the perfect complement to a complex pattern is no more complicated than a simple pattern of dots.

Take the time to knit up samples of your chart combinations. Not only are samples fun to knit, they provide the best means for determining whether patterns will work well together—and the samples will likely inspire you to think of other combinations. Another way to plan pattern combinations is to make photocopies of charts, cut them

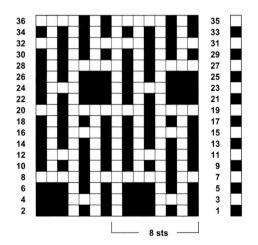

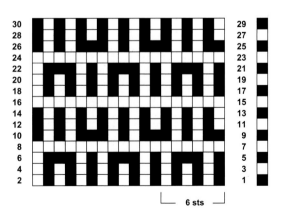

*These two patterns are very similar in scale and complexity and may therefore
be too repetitious to be used together.*

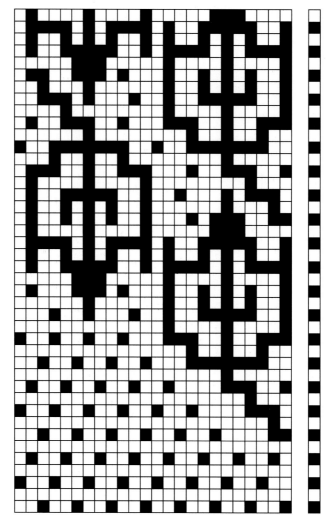

A simple dot pattern may be the best one to combine with a very complicated pattern.

out, and try them in different arrangements. As quick and appealing as this approach may be, you should still plan on knitting a sample to evaluate how the patterns look knitted up together. A chart made up of squares cannot take into account the small adjustments of shape that occur when squares are translated into combinations of slipped and knitted (and/or purled) stitches.

When knitting a garment with two or more slip-stitch patterns, plan the pattern changes carefully. A simple and effective approach is to coordinate the pattern transitions with the garment construction. For example, plan a change in pattern just before the shoulder as in the Coyote and Cactus Top (page 75), with the sleeves as in the Violets Underfoot Cardigan (page 78), at the cuff as in the Tulips Along the

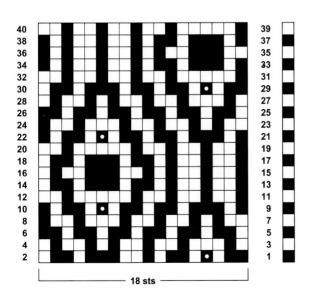

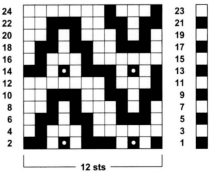

Patterns with similar shapes or rhythms will complement each other.

Nile Tunic (page 82), or just above the hem as in the Coyote and Cactus Top (page 75). Emphasizing garment construction in this way strengthens the overall design and results in a more striking piece. Alternatively, you can use a pattern to set off a particular area within a garment, such as a yoke or a sleeve, as in the Violets Underfoot Cardigan (page 78). Not only will this make for a more interesting garment, it will make for more engaging knitting.

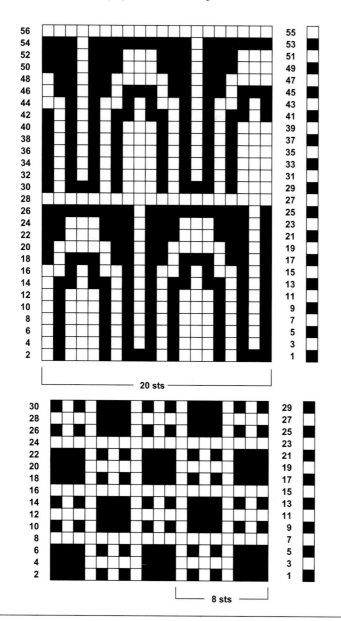

Patterns with different rhythms and sizes can also work well together.

CHAPTER 7

YARN OPTIONS

As with any multicolored pattern, yarn weight affects the look of a slip-stitch pattern. Thinner yarns make smaller motifs, heavier yarns make larger ones. Yarn weight also affects the number of times you can repeat a motif. Thinner yarns, which knit up with more stitches and rows to the inch, allow more pattern repeats within a given width or length of knitting. And thinner yarns that are smooth in texture will interpret a chart in a crisper image than will larger-scale yarns of similar texture. If you think of your pattern knitting as shapes developed on a grid, then selecting yarn weight is similar to adjusting the focus of a camera—the thinner the yarns, the smaller the increments of the grid and the sharper the image of the pattern. Try your favorite charts with yarns of different weights to investigate this effect.

Yarn construction and texture also affect a pattern. If a yarn is spun softly and left unplied, it interprets pattern shapes with softened edges—somewhat "out of focus", no matter what combination of colors and values you use. By contrast, clean, plied, unfuzzy yarns give a crispness to the edges. Highly textured yarns, especially ones that have halos of surface fibers, such

The small scale of sport-weight yarn interprets a slip-stitch pattern with crispness.

Bulky-weight yarn interprets patterns with a soft, somewhat "out-of-focus" quality.

Smooth-spun, plied yarns produce distinct pattern shapes.

Highly textured yarns such as mohair dramatically soften pattern definition.

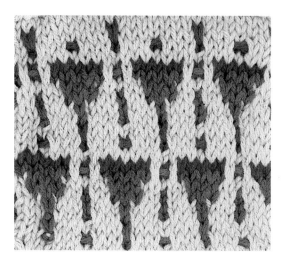

Cotton yarns have no halo to soften shapes.

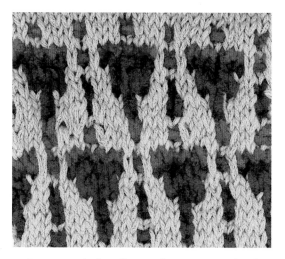

Cotton and chenille combine to give depth to the knitted surface.

CHAPTER 8

DESIGNING SLIP-STITCH PATTERNS

Designing your own slip-stitch patterns can be fun and rewarding! And it is not difficult once you understand the limits of slip-stitch designs. One such limitation is that no more than three stitches can be slipped at a time. More than that will cause the surface of the knitted fabric to corrugate. When slipping three stitches, take care to keep the carried yarn behind the stitches loose, or you may get puckering. Another limitation is that in order to slip a color it must be present in the row just worked, and it must be in the right place, ready to be slipped.

To make up a pattern, start with some graph paper with a grid of four or six squares to an inch (available at most stationery stores), some soft dark pencils, and a very large soft eraser. It helps in the beginning to think of only one element of your design—the dark (or positive) part of the chart. Limiting the changes in shapes to the dark rows will simplify the process and help you visualize it.

Changes in shapes can only be made with the color that is being worked. In other words, if you are knitting with black, you can add more black stitches but you cannot make fewer black stitches. That kind of change—fewer black stitches or more white stitches—will have to wait for a white row. These facts dictate the shapes you can and cannot make. All this will quickly become clear when you begin to plot your designs.

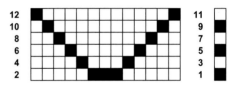

This V shape cannot be made with slip stitches because new dark stitches appear on light rows and new light stitches appear on dark rows.

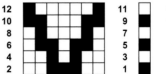

This V shape can be made with slip stitches.

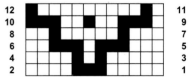

This V shape can be made with slip stitches but now a dark stitch must be added in the middle of the V to break up the 5 light stitches that would otherwise be slipped.

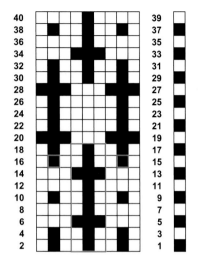

This chart will not work because new dark squares appear in light rows.

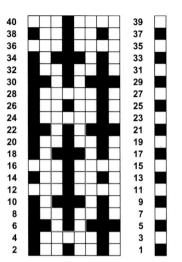

One solution to this problem is to move the shapes in the design closer together. Now new dark stitches appear only in dark rows.

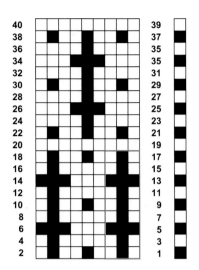

Another solution is to move the shapes in the design farther apart. New dark stitches appear only in dark rows.

As you develop a design, it is helpful to make a color key on the side of your chart to remind you which color is the working yarn in each row. Begin by arranging some black squares in a pattern on the graph paper. Keep the patterns simple at first; you can make them more elaborate later. When you work on a white row, decide which of the black pattern squares you wish to keep. When you work on the black row, decide where you want to add more black squares to your shapes. Once you have a pattern that you like, be sure to pick up your needles and try it out. Note any changes that actual knitting of the pattern dictates on your graph paper. Then begin experimenting with color and yarn combinations.

To make more complex designs, create a simple arrangement of black squares and make several copies of this shape. Then you can literally "cut and paste" your original shape into many pleasing groupings. Placing your shape in different positions may form repeated images or entirely new shapes.

Another design approach is to color relatively large dark shapes and refine them by erasing white squares. But remember to follow the dictates of slip-stitch patterns mentioned above.

Some people may find it easier to invent patterns on their needles. If you wish to try this approach, knit a few rows with a light yarn and then with a dark yarn begin knitting and slipping stitches. As your pattern develops, write it down by coloring squares on your graph paper. Whatever approach you use, creating patterns is a lot easier to do than you may think.

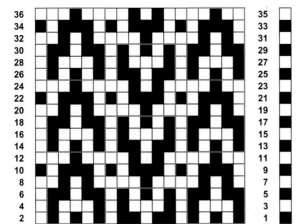

You can copy a simple arrangement of black squares and then cut and paste them into more complex designs.

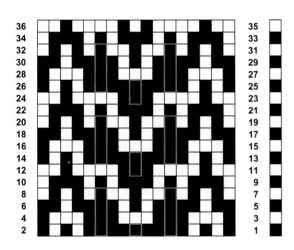

Once you develop a design, you can easily invent other designs by filling in more squares. Be sure to fill in dark squares only on dark rows or directly above other dark squares.

These flowers are offset, arranged in rows but not directly above one another.

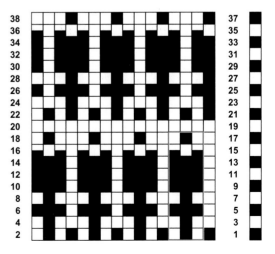

It is possible to manipulate shapes within the slip-stitch pattern by varying the technique a little bit. Changes made to an existing chart, though very simple, can effect distinct differences in shapes. For example, in the Bees in the Flower Garden Tunic (page 58), the flower shapes are compacted by simply knitting across the final even-numbered row of the pattern instead of knitting and slipping the stitches as in the odd row. In the Coyote and Cactus Top (page 75), the coyotes' noses are attenuated by a series of knit-two-togethers in the plain knit row just above the two stitches of the noses. On the next row this stitch is replaced by a backward loop increase that restores the original number of stitches.

There are ideas for patterns all around you—in the elements of decorative objects, fabrics, wallpaper, architectural shapes. Anything can be the start of a new pattern which you will then have to adapt to the "rules" of slip-stitch patterning. The shapes themselves don't have to be particularly complicated or elaborate. It is the complementary relationship of shapes and colors and textures that make a pattern a pleasure to look at—and to knit. And in this way a slip-stitch pattern is no different from any other complex color pattern technique—it's just *much easier* to knit!

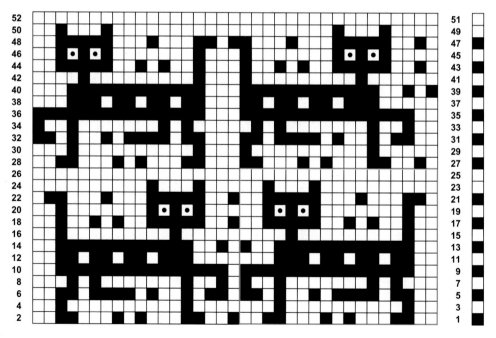

Once you have designed a shape that you like, you can use it in different ways to create an interesting all-over pattern. The cats were reversed in each row to add variety to the pattern.

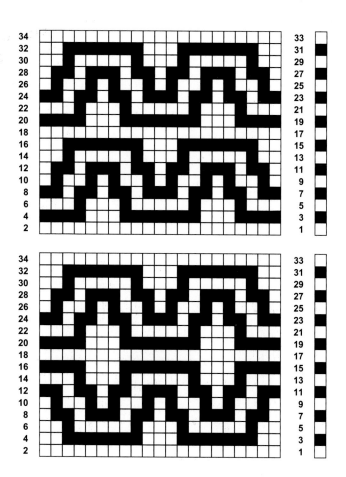

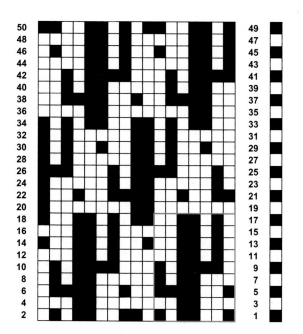

These cacti are both offset and interlocked. The cactus shapes are so close together that they overlap. If your pattern is arranged in this way, your repeats will form diagonals in the overall design.

Rearranging large units of your design can create entirely new shapes within your overall pattern.

CHAPTER 9

SLIP-STITCH CHARTS

Here are some charts to start you on your way to creating unique multicolored knitting the easy way. Many more charts can be found with the garment instructions in Chapter 10. Don't forget the dramatic effects texture and color changes can make.

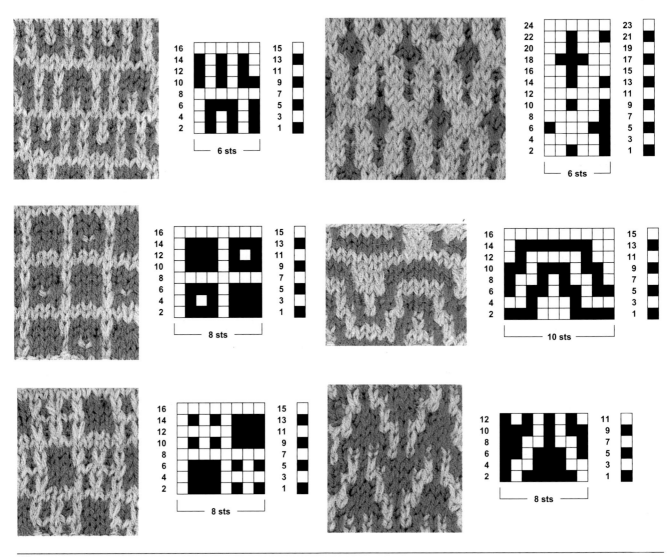

48

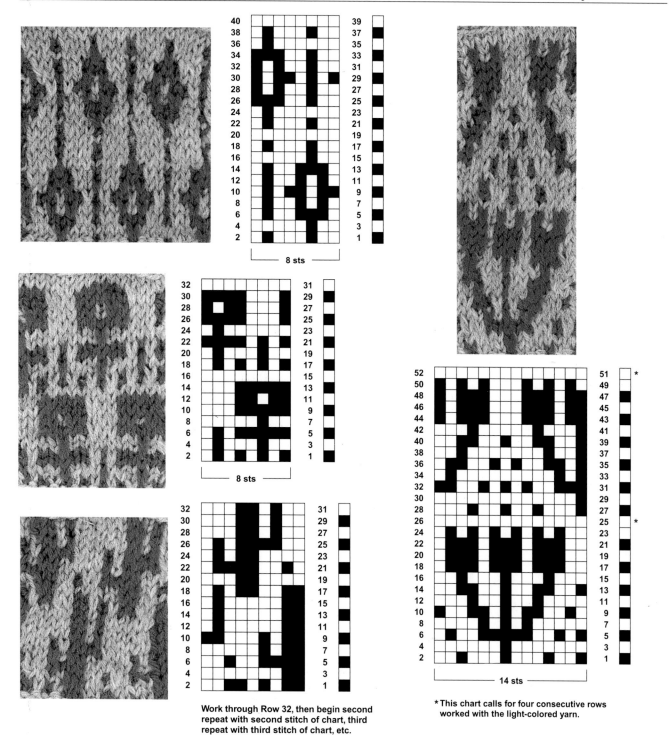

Work through Row 32, then begin second repeat with second stitch of chart, third repeat with third stitch of chart, etc.

*This chart calls for four consecutive rows worked with the light-colored yarn.

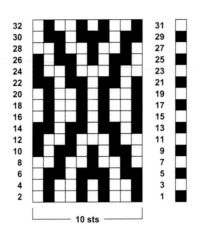

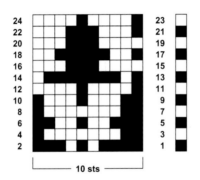

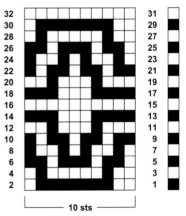

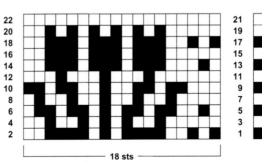

*This chart calls for four consecutive rows worked with the light-colored yarn.

CHAPTER 10

THE GARMENTS

The garments on the following pages illustrate some of the many ways to incorporate slip-stitch patterns in garment construction and ways that color can enhance a charted slip-stitch pattern. Complete instructions are provided for each garment. Follow the instructions as written or use them as a springboard for your own creative ideas.

Whenever possible, the charts for these garments are presented in color. So that you can photocopy (and enlarge) the charts in black and white, the colors are annotated with symbols. Large circles around these symbols denote stitches that are to appear as purl bumps (garter stitch) on the second row of two-row sequences. In black-and-white charts, the symbol for garter stitch is a solid dot.

The charts are numbered for back-and-forth knitting with odd-numbered rows labeled on the right and even-numbered rows on the left. If you are working in the round, read all rows from right to left. On many of the charts, color changes occur on the second row of a two-row sequence. These rows are to be worked in one direction only and are labeled on just one side (on the left for odd-numbered rows; on the right for even-numbered ones). For example, on Chart A of Baa Baa Black Sheep (page 56), row 17 is worked from right to left with white and row 18, the companion row, is worked from left to right with yellow.

Some of the more intricate color patterns involve color changes that do not repeat with the same frequency as the light/dark pattern repeat. These charts are printed as light and dark squares and the color sequences are listed next to the charts.

LONG-TAIL CAST-ON

Make a slip knot and place it on the right-hand needle, leaving a long tail. Place the thumb and index finger of your left hand between the two threads. Secure the long ends with your other three fingers. Hold your hand palm up and spread your thumb and index finger apart to make a V of the yarn around them. You have four strands of yarn, 1, 2, 3, and 4 (figure 1).

Place the needle under strand 1, from front to back. Place the needle over the top of strand 3 (figure 2) and bring the needle down through the loop around your thumb (figure 3). Drop the loop off your thumb and, placing your thumb back in the V configuration, tighten up the resulting stitch on the needle.

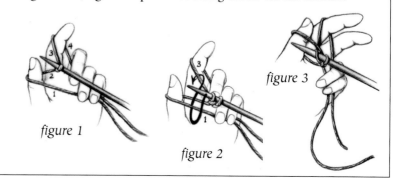

figure 1

figure 2

figure 3

BAA BAA BLACK SHEEP SWEATER

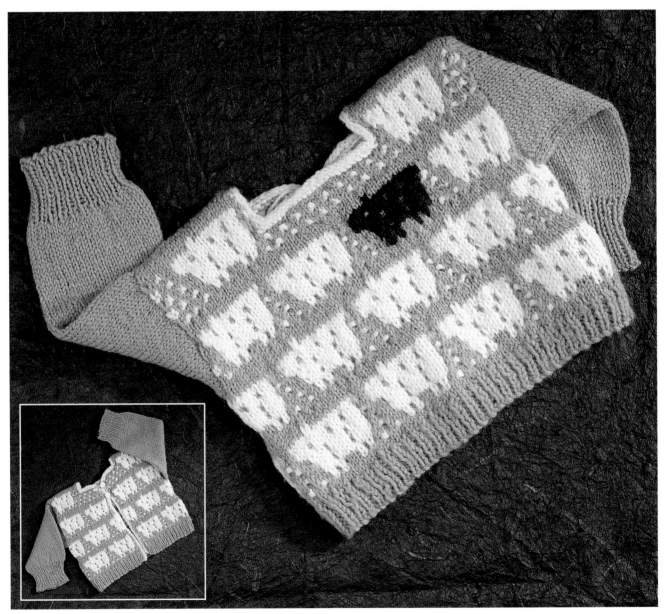

This sweater was worked with Dale of Norway Baby Ull (100% superwash merino;
192 yd [176 m]/50 g): #8523 Green, 2 (3) skeins; #0020 White, 2 (2) skeins;
#0083 Gray, #2203 Yellow, 1 (1) skein each.

BEES IN THE FLOWER GARDEN TUNIC

Finished Size: 21 (24, 26 ½)" (53.5 [61, 67.5] cm) chest circumference; to fit 18 months (3, 5 years). Sweater shown measures 21" (53.5 cm).

Yarn: Worsted weight: black, 200 (200, 300) g; red, yellow, jade, rose, magenta, 100 (100, 100) g each.

Needles: Body and Sleeves—Size 5 (3.75 mm): 16" or 24" (40 or 60 cm) circular (cir) and double-pointed (dpn); Ribbing—Size 3 (3.25 mm): 16" or 24" (40 or 60 cm) cir and dpn. Adjust needle sizes if necessary to obtain the correct gauge.

Notions: A few yd contrasting waste yarn; marker (m); four stitch holders; tapestry needle.

Gauge: 24 sts and 42 rnds = 4" (10 cm) in charted pattern on larger needle, blocked; 20 sts and 23 rnds = 4" (10 cm) in St st.

Body: With black, larger cir needle, and using invisible cast-on, CO 128 (144, 160) sts. Place m and join, being careful not to twist sts. Work St st for 1" (2.5 cm). *Picot turning rnd:* *YO, k2tog; rep from *. Work St st until piece measures ½ (¾, 1)" (1.3 [2, 2.5] cm) from picot rnd. Beg with Row 1, work charted pattern, working color changes as specified, and working purl bumps as indicated. Cont in patt until piece measures 7 ¾ (8 ¾, 10)" (19.5 [22, 25.5] cm) from picot rnd, ending 7 (7, 8) sts before m on last rnd. **Divide for front and back:** (RS) BO 14 (14, 16) sts for left armhole, work 50 (58, 64) sts for front and place on holder, BO 14 (14, 16) sts for right armhole, work to end. Place front sts on holder. Work rem body back and forth. **Back:** (WS) Cont in patt on 50 (58, 64) back sts until armhole measures about 5 ¾ (6 ½, 7)" (14.5 [16.5, 18] cm), ending on Row 20 or 40 of chart. *Next row:* Cont in patt, work 14 (17, 19) sts and place on holder for right shoulder, work next 22 (24, 26) sts and place on holder for back neck, work rem 14 (17, 19) sts and place on holder for left shoulder. **Front:** With WS facing, place 50 (58, 64) front sts on needle. Cont in patt until armhole measures 1 ¾ (2, 2)" (4.5 [5, 5] cm), ending with a WS row. *Divide for front neck opening:* Cont in patt, work 25 (29, 32) sts, join new yarn, work rem 25 (29, 32) sts. Working each side separately, cont in patt until arm-

---

INVISIBLE CAST-ON

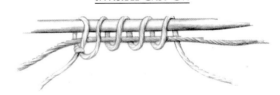

Make a slip knot and place it on the needle. Pull the waste yarn from left to right through the loop and lay it underneath the needle. Hold the slip knot and waste yarn in place with the left hand. Wind the main yarn round the needle plus waste yarn, over and away from you, under and towards you. As you get near the end of the waste yarn, pull a little more through. Make as many turns as you need stitches. Do not pull the waste yarn out until you are ready to pick up the loops to knit or slip them.

hole measures 3 ¼ (3 ½, 3 ½)" (8.5 [9, 9] cm). At each neck edge, BO 9 (9, 10) sts—16 (20, 22) sts rem each side. Cont in patt, dec 1 st each neck edge every other row 2 (3, 3) times—14 (17, 19) sts rem each side. Cont in patt until piece measures same length as back. **Shoulders:** With RS tog, BO shoulder sts tog (see page 94).

Sleeves: With black, larger cir needle, RS facing, and beg at inside corner of armhole notch, pick up and knit 58 (66, 70) sts around armhole from inner corner to inner corner. Do not join. Work these sts back and forth in St st while picking up 1 st at edge of body at each corner and knitting it tog with the first and last st of sleeve every other row until notch has been filled in. Change to

dpn, pm, and join, working rem sleeve in St st in the rnd, and *at the same time,* dec 1 st each side of m (2 sts dec'd) every 4 rnds 4 (0, 0) times then every 3 rnds 10 (17, 13) times then every 2 rnds 0 (0, 6) times as follows: K1, k2tog, knit to 3 sts before m, ssk, k1—30 (32, 32) sts rem. Cont even until sleeve measures 9 ¼ (10 ¼, 10 ½)" (23.5 [26, 26.5] cm), from pick-up row, or desired length to ribbing. With magenta and smaller dpn, work k1, p1 ribbing for 1 ½ (1 ½, 1 ¾)" (3.8 [3.8, 4.5] cm). With jade, work 2 more rnds ribbing. BO all sts loosely in ribbing.

Finishing: **Collar:** With magenta, smaller cir needle, WS facing, and beg at left front neck edge, pick up and knit 20 (23, 26) sts from left front neck edge, knit 22 (24, 26) sts from back holder, pick up and knit 20 (23, 26) sts from right front neck edge—62 (70, 78) sts. Work k1, p1 ribbing over 20 (23, 26) sts, inc 4 (6, 6) sts evenly across back neck keeping in ribbing, work ribbing over rem 20 (23, 26) sts—66 (76, 84) sts. Cont in ribbing for 2 ¼ (2 ½, 2 ¾)" (5.5 [6.5, 7] cm), ending with a WS row. With jade, knit 1 row, then work 1 row in ribbing. BO all sts in ribbing. **Hem:** Fold hem along picot rnd and carefully pull waste yarn out of invisible CO while slip stitching live sts in place loosely. With tapestry needle, weave in loose ends. Block.

black

flowers:
work in the following
color sequence:
Rows 10–15:
* magenta, rose, red; rep from *
Rows 30–35:
* red, magenta, rose; rep from *

yellow

jade

with specified color,
purl on even-numbered rounds
when working circularly;
knit on even-numbered rows
when working back and forth

8sts

Change flower color each pattern repeat.

ALL THE LITTLE HORSES PULLOVER

This sweater was worked with Plymouth Yarn Cascade 220 (100% wool; 220 yd [201 m]/100 g): #8895 Red (MC), 1 (2) skein(s). Brown Sheep Lamb's Pride Superwash Worsted Weight (100% wool; 100 yd [91 m]/50 g): #SW58 Navy Night, #SW31 Mallard, #SW64 Turf Green, 1 (1) skein each.

ALL THE LITTLE HORSES PULLOVER

Finished Size: 23 (30 ½)" (58.5 [77.5] cm) chest circumference; to fit 2–4 (6–8) years. Sweater shown measures 23" (58.5 cm).

Yarn: Worsted weight wool: red, 100 (200) g; navy, teal, bright green, 50 (50) g each.

Needles: Body and Sleeves—Size 6 (4 mm): 16" or 24" (40 or 60 cm) circular (cir) and double-pointed (dpn); Ribbing—Size 4 (3.5 mm): 16" or 24" (40 or 60 cm) cir and dpn. Adjust needle sizes if necessary to obtain the correct gauge.

Chart A

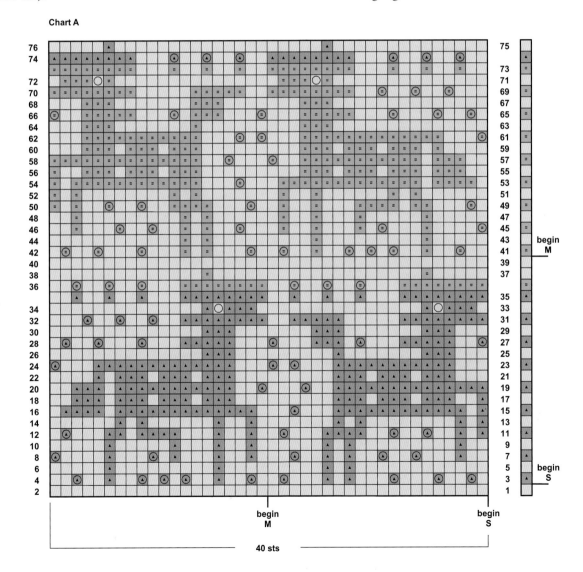

A WALK IN THE WOODS VEST

This vest was worked with Brown Sheep Nature Spun Sports Weight (100% wool; 184 yd [168 m]/50 g):
#720 Ash (MC), 2 (3) skeins. Plymouth Yarn Cleckheaton Tapestry (100% superwash wool; 109 yd [100 m]/50 g):
#3 multicolor, 2 (3) skeins. Cascade Lana D'Oro (50% wool, 50% alpaca; 110 yd [101 m]/50 g):
#216 dark blue, 2 (3) skeins; #214 teal, 1 (2) skein(s); #210 red, 1 (1) skein.

A Walk in the Woods Vest

Finished Size: 39 (43)" (99 [109] cm) bust/chest circumference, buttoned. Vest shown measures 39" (99 cm).

Yarn: Sport weight: gray, 100 (150) g. DK weight: multicolor, dark blue, 100 (150) g each; teal, 50 (100) g; red, 50 (50) g.

Needles: Body—Size 4 (3.5 mm): 32" (80 cm) circular (cir); Ribbing—Size 2 (2.75 mm): 32" (80 cm) cir; I-cord—Size 3 (3.25 mm): double pointed (dpn). Adjust needle sizes if necessary to obtain the correct gauge.

Notions: Four stitch holders; tapestry needle; one 1 ³/₄" (4.5-cm) pewter clasp.

Gauge: 25 sts and 46 rows = 4" (10 cm) in charted pattern on larger needle, blocked.

Body: With dark blue and larger cir needle, CO 215 (231) sts. Do not join. Change to smaller cir needle and work k1, p1 ribbing for 1 ¹/₄" (3 cm). Knit 1 row, inc 27 (33) sts evenly spaced—242 (264) sts. Change to larger cir needle. Knit 1 row. Purl 1 row. Beg charted patt, using gray for all light sts and specified color for dark sts, and work Rows 1–87, then work Rows 24–87 once (twice) more, then Rows 88–153 once—216 (280) rows total, and *at the same time,* when piece measures 10 ¹/₂ (14)" (26.5 [35.5] cm) from beg, ending with a WS row,

divide for front and back: Cont in patt, work 47 (51) sts for right front and place on holder, BO 26 sts for right armhole, work 96 (110) sts for back, place rem sts on holder. *Back:* Work back sts through Row 153 of chart—216 (280) rows total. *Next row:* With gray, p34 (38) sts for left shoulder, BO 32 (34) sts for back neck, p34 (38) sts for right shoulder. Place shoulder sts on holders. *Left front:* With RS facing, place 71 (77) left front sts on needle. Join yarn. BO 26 sts for left armhole. Cont in patt, work rem 47 (51) sts to last 2 sts, k2tog. Dec 1 st at neck edge in this manner every 4th row 11 (13) times—34 (38) sts rem. Cont in patt until piece measures same length as back. Place sts on holder. *Right front:* With WS facing, place 47 (51) sts on needle. Join yarn. Work as for left front, reversing neck shaping by working ssk decs at the beg of dec rows. *Shoulders:* With RS tog, BO shoulder sts tog (see page 94).

Finishing: *Front band and neckband:* With dark blue, dpn, RS facing, and beg at lower right front, work 3-st attached I-cord (see page 93) around the neckline, ending at the lower left front. With dark blue, work another attached I-cord in the same manner. Then with teal, work another attached I-cord in the same manner. *Armbands:* With dark blue and RS facing, work 3-st attached I-cord around armholes. With tapestry needle, weave in loose ends. Block. Sew clasp in place.

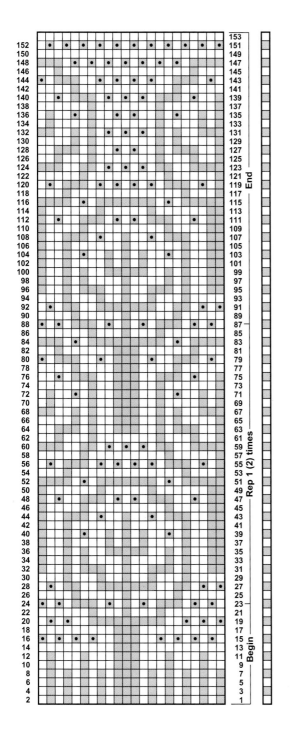

gray

dark color; work as specified

with specified color,
knit on even–numbered rows

39" Dark color sequence:
Rows 1–7: dark blue
Rows 8–19: multicolored
Rows 20–35: dark blue
Rows 36–47: multicolored
Rows 48–55: dark blue
Rows 56–75: teal
Rows 76–87: multicolored
Rows 24–31: dark blue
Rows 32–43: teal
Rows 44–63: multicolored
Rows 64–83: teal
Rows 84–87: multicolored
Rows 88–91: multicolored
Rows 92–107: teal
Rows 108–119: multicolored
Rows 120–127: red
Rows 128–143: multicolored
Rows 144–152: red
Row 153: gray

43" Dark color sequence:
Work Rows 1–87 once, rep
red highlighted area twice,
work Rows 88–153.

SPENCER'S VEST

This vest was worked with Brown Sheep Nature Spun Sports Weight (100% wool; 184 yd [168 m]/50 g): #308 Sunburst, #N13 Bluff, #N17 French Clay, 2 (2, 3) skeins each. Cascade Yarn Lana D'Oro (50% wool, 50% alpaca; 110 yd [101 m]/50 g): #214 Teal, 2 (2, 3) skeins; #216 Dark Blue, #212 Plum, 2 (2, 2) skeins each.

SPENCER'S VEST

Finished Size: 41 ¾ (45 ½, 49)" (106 [116, 124.5] cm) chest circumference. Vest shown measures 45 ½" (116 cm)

Yarn: Sport weight: gold, tan, pumpkin, 100 (100, 150) g each.

DK weight: teal 100 (100, 150) g; blue, dark plum, 100 (100, 100) g each.

Needles: Body—Size 5 (3.75 mm): 32" (80 cm) circular (cir); Ribbing—Size 3 (3.25 mm): 32" (80 cm) cir. Adjust needle sizes if necessary to obtain the correct gauge.

Notions: Marker (m); three stitch holders; tapestry needle.

Gauge: 22 sts and 42 rnds = 4" (10 cm) in charted pattern on larger cir needle, blocked.

Body: With blue and larger needle, CO 230 (250, 270) sts. Place m and join, being careful not to twist sts. Change to smaller needle. Work k1, p1 ribbing for 3 rnds. With teal, knit 1 rnd, then work k1, p1 ribbing until piece measures 2 ½ (2, 3)" (6.5 [5, 7.5] cm) from beg. With blue, knit 1 rnd. Change to larger needle. Beg with Row 3,

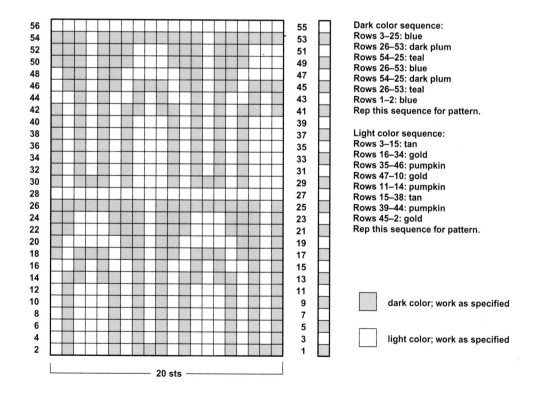

Dark color sequence:
Rows 3–25: blue
Rows 26–53: dark plum
Rows 54–25: teal
Rows 26–53: blue
Rows 54–25: dark plum
Rows 26–53: teal
Rows 1–2: blue
Rep this sequence for pattern.

Light color sequence:
Rows 3–15: tan
Rows 16–34: gold
Rows 35–46: pumpkin
Rows 47–10: gold
Rows 11–14: pumpkin
Rows 15–38: tan
Rows 39–44: pumpkin
Rows 45–2: gold
Rep this sequence for pattern.

▨ dark color; work as specified

☐ light color; work as specified

20 sts

work charted pattern, working color changes as specified. Cont in patt until piece measures 14 ½ (15 ½, 16)" (37 [39.5, 40.5] cm) from beg, ending 8 (9, 10) sts before m on last rnd and ending with an even-numbered rnd. **Divide for front and back:** BO 16 (18, 20) sts for left armhole, work 98 (106, 114) sts for front (99 [107, 115] sts total), BO 16 (18, 20) sts for right armhole, work to end. Place front sts on holder. Work rem body back and forth, **Back:** (WS) Cont in patt on 99 (107, 115) back sts, dec 1 st at each armhole edge every other row 5 (6, 7) times—89 (95, 101) sts rem. Cont in patt until armhole measures 9 (10, 10 ½)" (23 [25.5, 26.5] cm), ending with a WS row. *Next row:* Cont in patt, work 32 (33, 34) sts for right shoulder, k25 (29, 33) sts and place on holder for back neck, work 32 (33, 34) sts for left shoulder. Working the two sides separately, dec 1 st each neck edge twice—30 (31, 32) sts rem each side. Cont in patt until armhole measures about 9 ½ (10 ½, 11)" (24 [26.5, 28] cm), ending with Row 56 (28, 28) of chart. Place sts on holders. **Front:** With WS facing, place 49 (53, 57) front sts on needle, place center 7 st on holder, and place rem 49 (53, 57) front sts on needle. Working the two sides

separately, dec at armhole edges as for back and *at the same time,* dec 1 st each neck edge every 6 rows 14 (16, 18) times—30 (31, 32) sts rem each side. Cont in patt until piece measures same length as back, ending with Row 56 (28, 28) of chart. **Shoulders:** With RS tog, BO shoulder sts tog (see page 94).

Finishing: *Neckband:* With teal, smaller cir needle, RS facing, and beg at left shoulder, pick up and knit 62 (68, 72) sts along left front neck, pm, knit center st from holder, pm, pick up and knit 62 (68, 72) sts along right front neck and 5 sts along right back neck, k25 (29, 33) sts from back neck holder, and pick up and knit 5 sts along left back neck—150 (166, 178) sts. Place m and join. Work k1, p1 ribbing, dec before and after center st every other rnd as follows: work to 2 sts before 1st m, ssk, sl m, knit center st, sl m, k2tog, work to m. Cont in this manner until ribbing measures 1 ¼" (3.2 cm). With blue, BO all sts loosely. **Armbands:** With teal, smaller cir needle, RS facing, and beg at underarm, pick up and knit 116 (126, 132) sts around armhole. Work k1, p1 ribbing for 1" (2.5 cm). With blue, BO all sts loosely. With tapestry needle, weave in loose ends. Block.

COYOTE AND CACTUS TOP

This sweater was worked with Brown Sheep Cotton Fleece (80% cotton, 20% wool; 215 yd [197 m]/100g): #CW690 Alpine Lilac, 2 (3) skeins; #380 Dusty Sage, 1 (1) skein. Berroco Glacé (100% rayon ribbon; 75 yd [69 m]/50 g): #2360 Clover, 2 (3) skeins; #2361 Mulberry, 1 (2) skein(s).

COYOTE AND CACTUS TOP

Finished Size: 43 (54)" (109 [137] cm) bust circumference. Sweater shown measures 43" (109 cm).

Yarn: Worsted weight: lilac, 200 (300) g; sage, 100 (100) g.

Rayon ribbon: olive 100 (150) g; dark mauve, 50 (100) g.

Needles: Size 5 (3.75 mm): 16" and 32" (40 and 80 cm) circular (cir). Adjust needle size if necessary to obtain the correct gauge.

Notions: Marker (m); three stitch holders; size G (4.0 mm) crochet hook; tapestry needle.

Gauge: 22 sts and 46 rnds = 4" (10 cm) in charted pattern on cir needle, blocked; 20 sts = 4" (10 cm) in St st.

Pattern Stitch

Rnd/Row 1: *K5, p1; rep from *.
Rnds/Rows 2–6: Work in St st.
Rnd/Row 7: K2, *p1, k5; rep from *.
Rnds/Rows 8–12: Work in St st.

Body: With lilac, longer needle, and using the cable cast-on (see page 77), CO 216 (270) sts. Place m and join, being careful not to twist sts. Knit 1 rnd. Purl 1 rnd. With sage, knit 2 rnds. Beg with Row 1, work to end of Chart A. Then beg with Row 1, work Chart B. Then beg with Row 1, work Pattern st in lilac until piece measures 12 (13)" (30.5 [33] cm) from CO edge. ***Divide for front***

and back: Work across 108 (135) sts and place on holder for front. Work rem body back and forth. ***Back:*** Cont in patt on 108 (135) back sts until armhole measures 6" (15 cm). Beg with Row 1, work to end of Chart C 3 times, then work Rows 1–3. *Next row:* (WS) With lilac, p36 (48) sts for left shoulder, BO 36 (39) sts for back neck, p36 (48) rem sts for right shoulder. Place shoulder sts on holders. ***Front:*** With WS facing, place 108 (135) front sts on needle and work as for back through Row 7 of Chart C. *Next row:* (WS) Cont in patt, work 40 (52) sts, join new yarn, BO 29 (31) sts for front neck, work rem 40 (52) sts. Working the two sides separately and cont in patt, dec 1 st each neck edge 4 times—36 (48) sts rem each side. Cont in patt until front is same length as back. ***Shoulders:*** With *wrong sides* tog, BO shoulder sts tog (see page 94).

Sleeves: With lilac, shorter needle, RS facing, and beg at underarm, pick up and knit 72 sts around armhole. Place m and join. Knit 8 rnds. Then work Pattern st until piece measures 6" (15 cm) from pick-up rnd. Change to sage and knit 4 rnds. BO all sts.

Finishing: *Neck edging:* With lilac, RS facing, and beg at left shoulder, work 1 row of single crochet around neck edge. Then turn work and work 1 row of single crochet in the opposite direction, dec in center front and back as needed for the edging to lie flat. With tapestry needle, weave in loose ends. Block.

Chart A

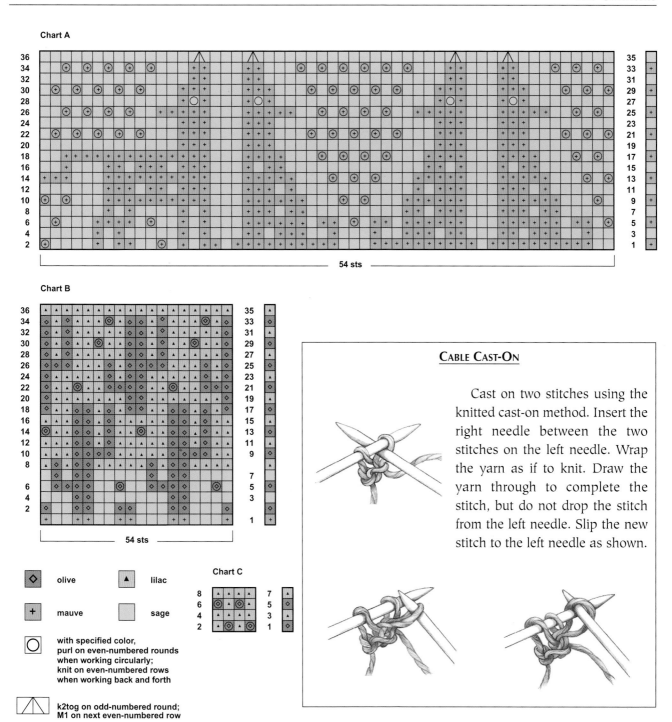

54 sts

Chart B

54 sts

◆ olive   ▲ lilac

+ mauve   ☐ sage

○ with specified color,
purl on even-numbered rounds
when working circularly;
knit on even-numbered rows
when working back and forth

△ k2tog on odd-numbered round;
M1 on next even-numbered row

Chart C

8		7
6		5
4		3
2		1

CABLE CAST-ON

Cast on two stitches using the knitted cast-on method. Insert the right needle between the two stitches on the left needle. Wrap the yarn as if to knit. Draw the yarn through to complete the stitch, but do not drop the stitch from the left needle. Slip the new stitch to the left needle as shown.

VIOLETS UNDERFOOT CARDIGAN

This cardigan was worked with Tahki Yarns Kashmir (75% Merino wool, 23% silk, 2% cashmere; 106 yd [97 m]/40 g): #968 teal, 4 (5, 5) balls; #993 olive, 4 (4, 4) balls; #985 green, 3 (3, 3) balls. Cascade Yarns Lana D'Oro (50% wool, 50% alpaca; 110 yd [101 m]/50 g): #213 medium purple, 3 (3, 4) skeins; #218 dark purple, 2 (2, 3) skeins; #221 light purple, 2 (2, 2) skeins.

Violets Underfoot Cardigan

Finished Size: 40 (43 ¼, 46 ½) " (101.5 [110, 118] cm) bust/chest circumference, buttoned. Sweater shown measures 43 ¼" (110 cm).

Yarn: Worsted weight: teal, 100 (200, 200) g; olive, 200 (200, 200) g; green, 150 (150, 150) g. DK weight: grape, 100 (100, 150) g, rose, 100 (100, 100) g; lavender, 150 (150, 200) g.

Needles: Body and Sleeves—Size 7 (4.5 mm): 32" (80 cm) circular (cir) and double-pointed (dpn); Ribbing—Size 4 (3.5 mm) 32" (80 cm) cir and dpn. Adjust needle sizes if necessary to obtain the correct gauge.

Notions: Marker (m); five stitch holders; tapestry needle; seven 1" (2.5-cm) buttons.

Gauge: 22 sts and 38 rnds = 4" (10 cm) in charted pattern on larger cir needle, blocked.

Chart A

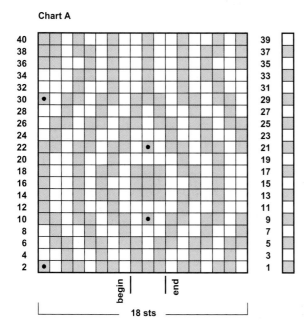

begin end

18 sts

Chart A color sequence

Rows 1–7: teal/lavender
Rows 8–11: teal/grape
Rows 12–17: teal/lavender
Rows 18–23: olive/lavender
Rows 24–27: olive/rose
Rows 28–35: olive/lavender
Rows 36–1: olive/grape
Rows 2–7: teal/grape
Rows 8–11: teal/lavender
Rows 12–17: teal/rose
Rows 18–23: green/rose
Rows 24–27: green/lavender
Rows 28–35: green/grape
Rows 36–1: green/lavender
Rows 2–7: teal/lavender
Rows 8–11: teal/rose
Rows 12–17: teal/lavender
Rows 18–23: olive/lavender
Rows 24–27: olive/grape
Rows 28–35: olive/lavender
Rows 36–1: olive/rose
Rows 2–7: teal/rose
Rows 8–11: teal/lavender
Rows 12–17: teal/grape
Rows 18–23: green/grape
Rows 24–27: green/lavender
Rows 28–35: green/rose
Rows 36–1: green/lavender
Rows 2–7: teal/lavender
Rows 8–11: teal/grape
Rows 12–17: teal//lavender
Rows 18–23: olive/lavender
Rows 24–27: olive/rose
Rows 28–35: olive/lavender
Rows 36–1: olive/grape
Rows 2–4: teal/grape

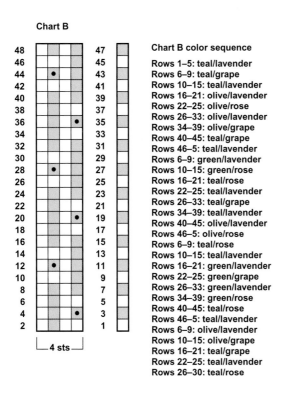

Chart B

48			47	
46			45	
44	•		43	
42			41	
40			39	
38			37	
36	•		35	
34			33	
32			31	
30			29	
28	•		27	
26			25	
24			23	
22			21	
20	•		19	
18			17	
16			15	
14			13	
12	•		11	
10			9	
8			7	
6			5	
4	•		3	
2			1	

└─ 4 sts ─┘

Chart B color sequence

Rows 1–5: teal/lavender
Rows 6–9: teal/grape
Rows 10–15: teal/lavender
Rows 16–21: olive/lavender
Rows 22–25: olive/rose
Rows 26–33: olive/lavender
Rows 34–39: olive/grape
Rows 40–45: teal/grape
Rows 46–5: teal/lavender
Rows 6–9: green/lavender
Rows 10–15: green/rose
Rows 16–21: teal/rose
Rows 22–25: teal/lavender
Rows 26–33: teal/grape
Rows 34–39: teal/lavender
Rows 40–45: olive/lavender
Rows 46–5: olive/rose
Rows 6–9: teal/rose
Rows 10–15: teal/lavender
Rows 16–21: green/lavender
Rows 22–25: green/grape
Rows 26–33: green/lavender
Rows 34–39: green/rose
Rows 40–45: teal/rose
Rows 46–5: teal/lavender
Rows 6–9: olive/lavender
Rows 10–15: olive/grape
Rows 16–21: teal/grape
Rows 22–25: teal/lavender
Rows 26–30: teal/rose

▨ dark color; work as specified

▢ light color; work as specified

• with specified color,
purl on even-numbered rounds
when working circularly;
knit on even-numbered rows
when working back and forth

Body: With olive and larger cir needle, CO 211 (229, 247) sts. Do not join. With teal and smaller cir needle, work twisted ribbing as follows:
Row 1: *K1 tbl, p1; rep from *, end k1 tbl.
Row 2: *P1, k1; rep from *, end p1.
Rep these 2 rows until piece measures 2" (5 cm), inc 2 sts evenly in last row—213 (231, 249). Change to larger cir needle. Beg as indicated with Row 3, work Chart A, changing colors and working purl bumps as specified, until piece measures 13 1/2 (14, 14 1/2)" (34.5 [35.5, 37] cm) from beg, ending with a WS row. **Divide for front and back:** Cont in pattern, work 51 (55, 60) sts for right front and place on holder, work 111 (121, 129) sts for back. Place rem 51 (55, 60) sts for left front on holder. **Back:** Cont in patt on 111 (121, 129) back sts until armhole measures 9 1/2 (10, 10)" (24 [25.5, 25.5] cm), ending with a WS row. *Next row:* Cont in patt, work 39 (42, 45) sts and place on holder for right shoulder, work 33 (37, 39) sts and place on another holder for back neck, work rem 39 (42, 45) sts and place on a third holder for left shoulder. **Left front:** With RS facing, place 51 (55, 60) left front sts on needle. Cont in patt until armhole measures 6 1/2 (7, 7)" (16.5 [18, 18] cm), ending with RS row. *Shape front neck:* (WS) BO 12 (13, 15) sts, work to end—39 (42, 45) sts rem. Cont in patt until piece measures same length as back, ending with a WS row. Place sts on holder. **Right front:** With WS facing, place 52 (55, 60) right front sts on needle. Work as for left front, reversing shaping.

Shoulders: With RS tog, BO shoulder sts tog (see page 94).

Sleeves: With teal, larger dpn, and beg at underarm, pick up and knit 104 (108, 108) sts around armhole. Place m and join. Beg with Row 1, work Chart B, changing colors and working purl bumps as specified, and *at the same time,* beg with Row 19 of the chart, dec 1 st each side of m (2 sts dec'd) as follows: k1, k2tog, work to last 3 sts, ssk, k1. Dec 2 sts in this manner every 6 rnds 12 times total, then every 8 rnds 8 times— 64 (68, 68) sts rem. Cont in patt until piece measures 17 (17 ½, 17 ½)" (43 [44.5, 44.5] cm), or desired length to ribbing. On next rnd, dec 20 sts evenly spaced—44 (48, 48) sts rem. Change to smaller dpn. With teal, work twisted ribbing for 14 rnds. With olive, BO all sts loosely.

Finishing: *Front band and neckband*: With teal, smaller cir needle, and beg at lower right front, pick up and knit 95 (99, 101) sts along right front edge and 30 (31, 33) sts along right neck edge, knit 33 (37, 39) sts from back neck holder, pick up and knit 30 (31, 33) sts along left neck edge, and 95 (99, 101) sts down left front edge— 283 (297, 307) sts. Work twisted ribbing for 3 rows. *Buttonholes:* On the next row, cont in patt and work 7 one-row buttonholes evenly spaced along the right front band. Work 3 more rows of twisted ribbing. With olive, BO all sts loosely. With tapestry needle, weave in loose ends. Block. Sew buttons to left front band.

ONE-ROW BUTTONHOLE

Work to where you want the buttonhole to begin, bring the yarn to the front, slip the next stitch purlwise, and then return the yarn to the back.

1. *Slip the next stitch. Then on the right needle, pass the second stitch over the end stitch. Repeat from * 2 (3, 4) times. Slip the last bound-off stitch to the left needle and turn the work.

2. Move the yarn to the back and use the cable cast-on to cast on 4 (5, 6) stitches as follows: *Insert the right needle between the first and second stitches on the left needle, draw up a loop, and place it on the left needle. Repeat from * 3 (4, 5) times. Turn the work.

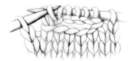

3. With the yarn in back, slip the first stitch from the left needle and pass the extra cast-on stitch over it to close the buttonhole. Work to the end of the row.

TULIPS ALONG THE NILE TUNIC

This sweater was worked with Brown Sheep Nature Spun Sports Weight (100% wool; 184 yd [168 m]/50 g): #750 White Port, #N92 Camel, 4 (4, 5) skeins each; #N76 Antique Turquoise, #N56 Meadow Green, 3 (3, 4) skeins each; #N81 Cranberry Fog, #N40 Grape Harvest, 2 (3, 3) skeins each.

TULIPS ALONG THE NILE TUNIC

Finished Size: 40 ½ (43 ¾, 47)" (103 [111, 119.5] cm) bust/chest circumference. Sweater shown measures 40 ½" (103 cm).

Yarn: Sport weight: white, camel, 200 (200, 250) g each; turquoise, green, 150 (150, 200) g each; cranberry, grape, 100 (150, 150) g each.

Needles: Body and Sleeves—Size 6 (4 mm): 16" and 32" (40 and 80 cm) circular (cir) and double-pointed (dpn); Hem—Size 4 (3.5 mm): 32" (80 cm) cir and dpn. Adjust needle sizes if necessary to obtain the correct gauge.

Notions: A few yd contrasting waste yarn; marker (m); three stitch holders; tapestry needle.

Gauge: 19 sts and 34 rnds = 4" (10 cm) in charted pattern on larger cir needle, blocked.

Note: Except for the hems, two strands of yarn are used throughout.

Body: With camel only, smaller cir needle, and using the invisible cast-on (see page 59), CO 192 (208, 224) sts. Place m and join, being careful not to twist sts. Work St st lining for 1" (2.5 cm). Change to larger cir needle, join white, and work the two yarns tog from here on. Purl 1 rnd. Knit 2 rnds. Beg with Row 1, work Chart A (using cranberry and grape tog as one yarn and green and turquoise tog as one yarn) until piece measures 15 (16 ½, 16 ½)" (38 (42, 42)

cm) from purl ridge, ending 5 (7, 9) sts before m on last rnd. ***Divide for front and back:*** BO 10 (14, 18) sts for left armhole, work 85 (89, 93) sts for front (86 [90, 94] sts total), BO 10 (14, 18) sts for right armhole, work to end. Place front sts on holder. Work rem body back and forth. ***Back:*** Work 86 (90, 94) back sts in patt until armhole measures 9 ½ (10, 10)" (24 (25.5, 25.5) cm), ending with a WS row. *Next row:* With camel/white, work 28 (29, 30) sts for right shoulder, BO 30 (32, 34) sts for back neck, work rem 28 (29, 30) sts for left shoulder. Place shoulder sts on holders. ***Front:*** Place 86 (90, 94) front sts on needle. Cont in patt until armhole measures 7 (7 ½, 7 ½)" (18 (19, 19) cm), ending with a WS row. *Next row:* Cont in patt, work 28 (29, 30) sts, join new yarn, work 30 (32, 34) sts and place on holder for front neck, work rem 28 (29, 30) sts. Working each side separately, cont in patt until piece measures same length as back. ***Shoulders:*** With RS tog, BO shoulder sts tog (see page 94).

Sleeves: With camel/white and larger cir needle, pick up and knit 95 (101, 101) sts around armhole from inner corner to inner corner. Do not join. Beg Chart B, working back and forth across these sts while picking up 1 st at edge of body at each corner and knitting it tog with first and last st of sleeve every row until armhole notch is filled in. Place m and join. Cont in patt, work rem of sleeve in the rnd, and *at the same time,* dec 1 st each side of m (2 sts dec'd total) every 5 rnds 28 (20, 20) times then every 4 rnds 0 (11, 11) times as follows: k1, k2tog, knit to last 3 sts, ssk, k1—39 sts rem. Cont in patt until sleeve measures 17 (17 ½, 18)" (43 [44.5, 46] cm) from pick-up row, or 1 ½" (3.8 cm) less than desired length, changing to dpn when necessary. With camel/white, knit 2 rnds. Work Chart C. With camel/white, knit 1 rnd, then purl 1 rnd. Break off white and change to lining dpn. With camel only, work St st lining for 1" (2.5 cm). Place live sts on holder.

Finishing: *Hem:* Fold lining along purl ridge and carefully pull waste yarn out of invisible CO while slip stitching live sts in place loosely. *Cuffs:* Fold lining along purl ridge and slip stitch live sts in place. *Neckband:* With camel/white, dpn, and beg at right shoulder seam, work 2-st attached I-cord (see page 93) around neck edge. With tapestry needle, weave in loose ends. Block.

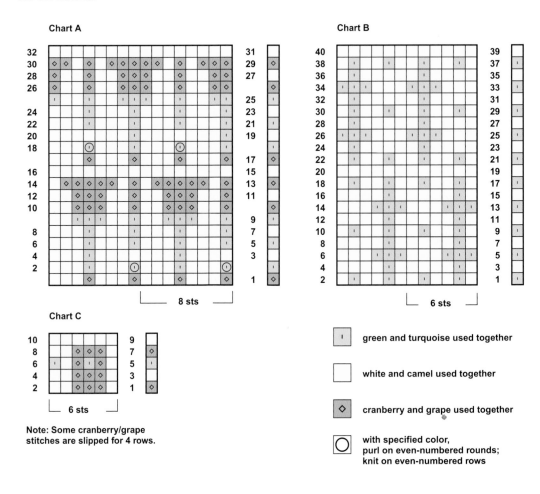

Chart A

8 sts

Chart B

6 sts

Chart C

6 sts

Note: Some cranberry/grape stitches are slipped for 4 rows.

| | green and turquoise used together |

| | white and camel used together |

| ◇ | cranberry and grape used together |

| ◯ | with specified color, purl on even-numbered rounds; knit on even-numbered rows |

EVENING OF FALLING STARS SOCKS

These socks were worked with Tahki Yarns Stahl Wolle Hobby Kids (60% acrylic, 40% superwash wool; 120 yd [110 m]/50 g): #4662 Multicolored Black, 1 ball. Tahki Yarns Stahl Wolle Hobby (60% superwash wool, 40% acrylic; 137 yd [125 m]/50 g): #4814 Bordeaux, 1 ball. Brown Sheep Nature Spun Sports Weight (100% wool; 184 yd [168 m]/50 g): #N75 South Pacific Blue, 1 skein.

Finished Size: 10" (25.5 cm) from heel to toe; 7" (18 cm) from cuff to top of heel. To fit a medium/large adult foot.

Yarn: Sport weight: multicolored, red, blue, 50 g each.

Needles: Leg and Foot—Size 3 (3.25 mm): set of four double-pointed (dpn). Heel and Toe—Size 2 (2.75 mm): set of four dpn. Adjust needle sizes if necessary to obtain the correct gauge.

Notions: Marker (m); a few yd waste yarn; tapestry needle.

Gauge: 14 sts and 21 rnds = 2" (5 cm) in charted pattern on larger needles, blocked.

Cuff: With multicolored and larger dpn, *loosely* CO 48 sts. Divide sts evenly onto 3 dpn. Place m and join, being careful not to twist sts. Work k2, p2 ribbing for 2 rnds. With red, knit 1 rnd, then work k2, p2 ribbing for 1" (2.5 cm). With blue, knit 2 rnds.

Leg: Beg with multicolored and Row 1, work chart, alternating multicolored and blue every 2 rnds, until leg measures 7" (18 cm), or desired length to top of heel. Break both yarns. Sl 12 sts from needle #3 to needle #1.

Heel: With multicolored, knit across 12 sts, sl m, and knit across next 12 sts. Sl rem 24 sts of instep onto waste yarn. Change to smaller dpn. Turn.

Heel flap:

Row 1: Sl 1, purl to end. Turn.

Row 2: With blue, *sl 1, k1; rep from *. Turn.

Rep these 2 rows, alternating colors every 2 rows until heel flap measures 2 ¼"

(5.5 cm), or desired length, ending with multicolored and a RS row.

Turn heel:

Row 1: With multicolored, sl 1, purl to 3 sts beyond m, p2tog, p1. Turn.

Row 2: Sl 1, k7 (3 sts beyond m), sl 1, k1, psso, k1. Turn.

Row 3: Sl 1, purl to 1 st before gap, p2tog, p1. Turn.

Row 4: Sl 1, knit to 1 st before gap, sl 1, k1, psso, k1. Turn.

Cont in this manner until all heel sts have been used. Change to larger dpn.

Heel gussets: With multicolored and RS facing, pick up and knit 1 st for every slipped edge st along the left side of the heel flap. Place 24 instep sts on a spare needle, and with needle #2, knit across these sts. With needle #3, pick up and knit 1 st for every slipped edge st along the right side of the heel flap, and then work across heel sts to m, sl m. *Dec rnd:* Transfer rem 8 heel sts to needle #1, then knit across picked-up sts to last 3 sts, k2tog, k1. With

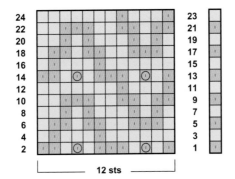

multicolored

blue

with specified color,
purl on even-numbered rounds

12 sts

needle #2, knit across instep sts. With needle #3, k1, sl 1, k1, psso, knit to m. Change to blue and knit 1 rnd. Rep the last 2 rnds, alternating colors every 2 rnds, until 12 sts rem each on needle #1 and needle #3. Beg with next color and Row 1 or 3 of chart, work until foot measures 8" (20.5 cm), or desired length from back of heel, alternating colors every 2 rnds and ending with 2 rnds of blue. Change to smaller dpn.

Toe: With red, knit across needle #1 to last 3 sts, k2tog, k1. On needle #2, k1, sl 1, k1, psso, knit to last 3 sts, k2tog, k1. On needle #3, k1, sl 1, k1, psso, knit to end. Knit 1 rnd even. Rep these 2 rnds until 8 sts rem on needle #2 and 4 sts each on needle #1 and needle #3—16 sts total. Cut yarn, leaving a 12" (30.5 cm) tail.

Finishing: With yarn threaded on tapestry needle, use kitchener st to graft toe sts tog. Weave in loose ends. Block.

KITCHENER STITCH

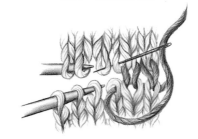

1. Bring yarn needle through the first front st as if to purl, leaving the st on needle.

2. Bring yarn needle through the first back st as if to knit, and then sl this st off needle. Bring yarn needle through next back st as if to purl, leaving the st on needle.

3. Bring yarn needle through the same front st as if to knit, and then sl this st off needle. Bring needle through the next front st as if to purl, again leaving the st on needle.

4. Bring yarn needle through the first back st as if to purl, sl that st off, and then bring yarn needle through the next back st as if to knit, leaving it on needle. Rep steps 3 and 4 until no sts remain.

NAUGHTY KITTENS HAT AND MITTENS

*These pieces were worked with Brown Sheep Nature Spun Sports Weight (100% wool; 184 yd [168 m]/50 g):
#N36 China Blue, #N65 Sapphire, #N76 Antique Turquoise, 1 skein each.*

Finished Size: *Hat:* 17" (43 cm) circumference; to fit a medium child's head. *Mittens:* 6" (15 cm) around by 6 ¼" (16 cm) long, excluding ribbing; to fit a small child's hand.

Yarn: Sport weight: periwinkle, purple, turquoise, 50 g each.

Needles: Size 5 (3.75 mm): 16" (40 cm) circular (cir) and set of four double-pointed (dpn). Adjust needle size if necessary to obtain the correct gauge.

Notions: Marker (m); tapestry needle; a few yd contrasting waste yarn; stitch holder.

Gauge: 24 sts and 42 rnds = 4" (10 cm) in charted pattern, blocked.

HAT

With purple and cir needle, CO 102 sts loosely. Place m and join, being careful not to twist sts. Work k1, p1 ribbing for 5 rnds. With periwinkle, work ribbing for 4 rnds. With purple, work ribbing for 4 rnds. With turquoise, knit 4 rnds. Beg with Row 1, work Chart A. Knit 4 rnds with turquoise, 2 rnds with purple, 2 rnds with periwinkle, 2 rnds with purple, and 8 rnds (or to desired length) with periwinkle.

Dec for top:

Rnd 1: K1, *k2, k2tog; rep from *, end k1—77 sts.

Rnd 2: Knit.

Rnd 3: K1, *k1, k2tog; rep from *, end k1—52 sts.

Rnd 4: Knit.

Rnd 5: *K2tog; rep from *—26 sts.

Break yarn, thread tail through rem sts, draw up, and fasten off.

Finishing: With purple, make pom-pom (see page 92) and attach to top of hat. With tapestry needle, weave in loose ends. Block.

MITTENS

Right Mitten: With purple and dpn, CO 40 sts loosely. Arrange sts evenly over 3 needles, pm, and join, being careful not to twist sts. Work k1, p1 ribbing for 5 rnds. *With periwinkle, work 4 rnds ribbing, then with purple, work 4 rnds ribbing. Rep from * once. With turquoise, knit 2 rnds. Rearrange sts so that 20 sts are on needle #1 (for back of hand) and 10 sts each on needles #2 and #3 (for palm). Work back sts according to Chart B and palm sts according to Chart C. On Row 14 of Chart B, mark thumb placement on first 7 palm sts by knitting these sts with waste yarn, and then placing them back on the left nee-

Chart A

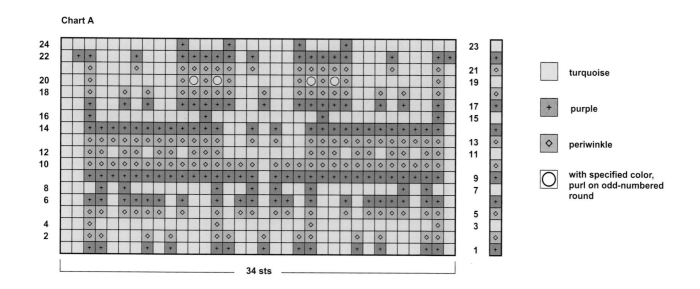

turquoise

+ purple

◇ periwinkle

◯ with specified color, purl on odd-numbered round

34 sts

Chart B

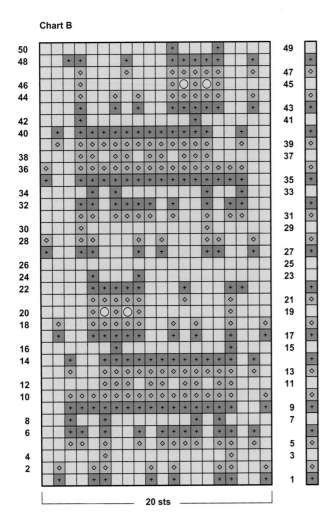

20 sts

Chart C

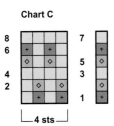

4 sts

dle. Cont in patt to end of chart. Then knit 2 rnds with turquoise, followed by 2 rnds with purple. With periwinkle, *k1, sl 1; rep from * for 2 rnds, then knit 2 rnds. With purple, *k1, sl 1; rep from * for 2 rnds. Change to periwinkle and knit 1 rnd. On next rnd, *k2tog; rep from *—20 sts rem. Break yarn, thread tail through rem sts, draw up, and fasten off. ***Thumb:*** Carefully remove waste yarn and place bottom 7 sts on one needle and top 6 sts on another needle. With turquoise, knit the bottom 7 sts onto needle #1. With needle #2, pick up and knit 3 sts in the gap between the two needles, and knit 3 of the 6 top sts. With needle #3, knit the rem 3 top sts and pick up and knit 2 sts in the rem gap—18 sts (7 sts on needle #1, 6 sts on needle #2, and 5 sts on needle #3). Place m and join. Knit 1 rnd. Beg with purple, cont palm patt until thumb measures 1 ½" (3.8 cm). With turquoise, knit 2 rnds. With periwinkle, knit 1 rnd, then *k2tog; rep from * for 1 rnd. Break yarn, thread tail through rem sts, draw up, and fasten off.

Left Mitten: Work as for right mitten, but begin Chart B on Row 27, working Rnds 28–50, then 2 rnds turquoise, then Rows 1–26 to reverse cat images, and work thumb over last 7 palm sts.

REINDEER IN THE SNOW HAT

This hat was worked with Cascade Yarns Lana D'Oro (50% wool, 50% alpaca; 110 yd [101 m]/50 g): #210 Rose, #201 White, 1 (1) skein each. Plymouth Yarn Cleckheaton Tapestry (100% superwash wool; 109 yd [100 m]/50 g): #6 multicolored, 1 (1) skein.

Finished Size: 17 ¼ (20 ¾)" (44 [53] cm) circumference; to fit a medium child's (adult's) head.

Yarn: DK weight: rose, white, multicolored, 50 (50) g each.

Needles: Size 4 (3.5 mm): 16" (40 cm) circular (cir) and double-pointed (dpn). Adjust needle size if necessary to obtain the correct gauge.

Notions: A few yd contrasting waste yarn; marker (m); tapestry needle.

Gauge: 22 sts and 44 rnds = 4" (10 cm) in charted pattern, blocked.

With rose, cir needle, and the invisible cast-on (see page 59), CO 95 (114) sts. Place m and join, being careful not to twist sts. Work St st for 2 ½ (3)" (6.5 [7.5] cm). Purl 1 rnd, then knit 2 rnds. With multicolored, knit 2 (3) rnds. Beg with Row 1, work to end of Chart A. With multicolored, knit 3 rnds, dec 2 (0) sts evenly spaced on last rnd—93 (114) sts rem. Work Chart B for a total of 10 (18) rnds, dec 1 (2) sts on last rnd—92 (112) sts. ***Dec for top:*** With multicolored, *k2, k2tog; rep from *—69 (84) sts. Knit 1 rnd, dec 1 (0) sts—68 (84) sts. *K2, k2tog; rep from *—51 (63) sts. Knit 1 rnd. Change to rose. [*K1, k2tog; rep from * for 1 rnd, then knit 1 rnd] once (twice)—34 (28) sts. On next rnd, *k2 tog; rep from *—17 (14) sts. Break yarn, thread tail through rem sts, draw up, and fasten off.

Finishing: Fold hem along purl ridge, carefully pull waste yarn out of invisible CO, while slip stitching live sts in place loosely. With rose, make pom-pom and attach to top of hat. With tapestry needle, weave in loose ends. Block.

Chart A

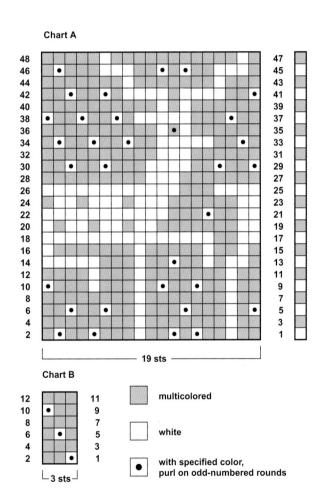

└─ 19 sts ─┘

Chart B

└─ 3 sts ─┘

multicolored

white

● with specified color, purl on odd-numbered rounds

Pom-pom

Cut a piece of heavy cardboard as wide as you want the diameter of your pom-pom to be—3" (7.5 cm) for a medium pom-pom.

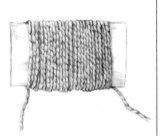

Wrap yarn 40 to 50 times around the cardboard—more if your yarn is finer than worsted weight, or if your pom-pom is to be very large.

Slip the loops off the cardboard, tie them tightly in the center, and cut the loops.

Shake the pom-pom to fluff it out, and trim evenly.

GLOSSARY

I-CORD

With dpn, CO desired number of sts. *Without turning the nee- dle, slide the sts to the other end of the needle, pull the yarn around the back, and knit the sts as usual; rep from * for desired length.

ATTACHED I-CORD

As I-cord is knit-ted, attach it to the garment as follows: With garment RS facing and using a separate ball of yarn and cir nee-dle, pick up the desired number of sts

along the garment edge. Slide these sts down the needle so that the first picked-up st is near the opposite needle point. With dpn, CO desired number of I-cord sts. Knit across the I-cord to the last st, then knit the last st tog with the first picked-up st on the garment, and pull the yarn behind the cord. Knit to the last I-cord st, then knit the last I-cord st tog with the next picked-up st. Cont in this manner until all picked-up sts have been used.

Note: When working attached I-cord, as in all picked-up edge finishes, do not pick up every st. Work the edg-ing for about 2" (5 cm), then lay the piece flat to make sure that the cord lies flat along the edge—if not pull out the necessary sts and rework, picking up more or fewer sts along the garment edge, as needed.

M1 INCREASE

With left needle tip, lift the strand between the last knitted stitch and the first stitch on the left needle, from front to back.

Knit the lifted loop through the back.

BINDING OFF SHOULDER STITCHES TOGETHER

Place the front and back shoulder stitches onto two separate needles. Hold them in your left hand with the sepcified (usually right) sides of the knitting facing together. In your right hand, take another needle and insert the right-hand needle into the first stitch on each of the left-hand needles and knit them as one stitch. Knit the next stitch the same way. You now have two stitches on the right-hand needle. Pass the first stitch over the second stitch. Repeat until only one stitch remains on the right-hand needle. Cut the yarn and pull the tail through last stitch.

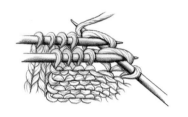

SSK DECREASE
This is a left-slanting decrease.

Slip two stitches individually knitwise.

Insert the point of the left needle into the front of the two slipped stitches and knit them together through the back loop with the right needle.

ABBREVIATIONS

beg	beginning; begin; begins	M1	make one	tbl	through back loop
BO	bind off	p	purl	tog	together
CC	contrasting color	patt(s)	pattern(s)	WS	wrong side
cm	centimeter(s)	pm	place marker	wyf	with yarn in front
CO	cast on	psso	pass slip stitch over	yd(s)	yard(s)
cir	circular	p2tog	purl two stitches together	yo	yarn over
cont	continue	rem	remaining	*	repeat starting point (i.e., repeat from *)
dec(s)	decrease(s); decreasing	rep	repeat		
g	gram	rnd(s)	round(s)	( )	alternate measurements and/or instructions
inc	increase; increasing	RS	right side		
k	knit	sc	single crochet	[ ]	instructions that are to be worked as a group a specified number of times, or alternate measurements
k tbl	knit through back of loop	skp	sl 1, k1, psso		
k2tog	knit two stitches together	sl	slip		
m	marker(s)	ssk	slip, slip, k 2 sl sts tog		
MC	main color	st(s)	stitch(es)		
mm	millimeters	St st	stockinette stitch		

INDEX